50 Days to EMBRACING (and enjoying) Who God Says YOU ARE

Eric Geiger & Eden Geiger

wander™
An imprint of
Tyndale House
Publishers

Visit Tyndale online at tyndale.com.

Visit Eric Geiger online at ericgeiger.com.

50 Days to Embracing (and Enjoying) Who God Says You Are

Designed by Jacqueline L. Nuñez

For information about special discounts for bulk purchases, please contact Tyndale House Publishers at csresponse@tyndale.com, or call 1-800-323-9400.

ISBN 979-8-4005-0959-9

Printed in the United States of America

32 31 30 29 28 27 26
7 6 5 4 3 2 1

Dedicated to Kaye Geiger—mentor, teacher, tutor, friends' tutor, Uber driver, chef, Bible-study host, Bible teacher, counselor, problem-solver, comedian, party organizer, clothing maker, nurse, stylist, shopping assistant, hairstylist, and the list goes on.

But top of the list is wife and mom.

You are the best! You are such a gift to us. We love you!

Contents

WEEK THREE:

God Has Made Me Right with Himself

WEEK FOUR:

I Am with God and for God

WEEK FIVE:

I Should Not Always Fit In

WEEK SIX:

I Represent Christ

WEEK SEVEN:

God Is for Me

A Note from Eric and Eden

We are so honored to go on this journey with you—a journey of embracing and enjoying who God says we are.

If you are already a Christ follower, the Bible is loaded with descriptions of your new identity. Studying what Scripture says about you will encourage you, change you, and challenge you. That is our story!

If you are not yet a Christ follower, you will get to see what Christians believe, and you can consider what God is offering you. We love that you are reading this!

Each day you will see the daily devotional in two parts. The first part is written by Eric, and the second part is by Eden. Eric is Eden's dad and a pastor who has spent years of his life leading groups of high school students. Eden is a teenager, and she is currently doing her best to apply all of this to her own life—just like you.

When I (Eric) started following Christ my senior year in high school, I struggled with really understanding that I was brand new and forgiven, that I had a new identity. I was embarrassed about things I had done and struggled with guilt. Studying my new identity, as described in Scripture, helped me so much, and I know the Scripture will help you too.

I (Eden) have struggled with where to place my identity. I have been tempted to find identity in my struggles, like having dyslexia or wrestling with anxiety. I have been tempted to find my identity in things I want to accomplish or good things I do, but that only puts more pressure on me and does not give me joy. When I remember who Christ has declared me to be, I have more joy, and I want that for you too!

We encourage you to read one devotional a day for the next fifty days. Don't read more than one per day because we hope you will reflect on what you read throughout the day. If you miss a day, just pick back up. If it takes longer than fifty days for you to complete it, that's okay!

We also included a memory verse for each week and a few questions at the end of each day. These will help you reflect on what God is teaching you, and you could also use the discussion questions if you are reading with friends or a Bible study group.

Let's go!

Memory Verse

You made all the delicate, inner parts of my body
and knit me together in my mother's womb.
Thank you for making me so wonderfully complex!
Your workmanship is marvelous—how well I know it.

PSALM 139:13-14

WEEK ONE

God Designed Me with Great Care

You made all the delicate, inner parts of my body
and knit me together in my mother's womb.
Thank you for making me so wonderfully complex!
Your workmanship is marvelous—how well I know it.

PSALM 139:13-14

DAY 1

I Am Wonderfully Knit Together

Eric

If you long for the day when you will be able to drive yourself to school or to Starbucks or to a friend's house, you are not alone. Getting into a car—without your parents or a driving instructor—and driving down the road is a major milestone. If the car you want to drive (or are driving) is like most cars, it has around 30,000 parts and takes manufacturers 18 to 35 hours to make. You look at the car of your dreams and think, *This thing is awesome*. You never think, *This car just happened*. The fact that the car has been designed means it had a designer.

In a similar way, your incredibly intricate body points to a much greater Designer. It didn't come into existence by chance. Just think about the complexity of a car versus the complexity of the human body:

The car: 30,000 parts
Your body: 30,000,000,000,000 (30 trillion) cells

The car: 35 hours in the factory (on the high end)
You: 6,570 hours in the womb (or nine months)

God spoke the world into existence and created everything in six days. He said, "Let there be light," and there was light (see Genesis 1:3). But with you, He took extra time. He did not just speak. He knit you together.

Just as your dream car points to a designer, you point to a Designer. God designed and created you, which means you are worth much more than a car. Not only because you have more cells and took longer to make, but because your Maker is God Himself. Your dream car will be worth less five years from now. That's called "depreciation," a word you'll probably hear in some economics class. You don't depreciate, though. Your worth remains because the One who created you set His image on you. (We will talk more about this tomorrow!)

Eden

For a teenager growing up in the social media era, the comparison game is real. Body image is a major concern for many of us. It's challenging not to fixate on how we appear to others or how we stack up against people with tons of likes on Instagram or those stunning models. I have felt judged based on my style, my fitness, and even my height. It's easy for our self-esteem to take a hit, and I've found myself wondering, *Why do I look like this?!*

"Ten years from now, no one will remember that pimple," a friend might say. True, but today is today, not ten years from now! I need something to help me right now.

Psalm 139 helps me remember this. God is the One who made

me, and He never makes mistakes. What He thinks of me is far more important than anyone else's opinion. Next time you feel insecure about your appearance or abilities, remind yourself that you've been wonderfully made by the Creator of the universe!

Reflection & Discussion Time

- What causes people (maybe even you) to have a low view of yourself? Of your body?
- How does Psalm 139 challenge you and help you think differently about who God made you to be?

Then God said, "Let us make human beings in our image, to be like us. They will reign over the fish in the sea, the birds in the sky, the livestock, all the wild animals on the earth, and the small animals that scurry along the ground."

GENESIS 1:26

DAY 2

I Am Made in His Image

Eric

The word *genesis* means "beginning," so the book of Genesis is the book of beginnings, including the beginning of people. The first words of Genesis are "In the beginning God created . . ." God was there in the beginning, meaning He has no beginning because He has always been. He is not like us, because all of us have a beginning—a date we were born into this world. We are the created; He is the Creator.

Throughout Genesis 1, God says that what He created was good:

- The light: good (verse 4)
- The land and seas: good (verse 10)
- The sun, moon, and stars: good (verses 16-18)
- The animals: good (verse 25)

A musician often plays his best song at the end of the concert. An artist often displays her best piece at the end of the exhibit. And

God saved His best work, His most creative act for the end. The crowning work of God's creation was making people. "Then God looked over all he had made, and he saw that it was *very good*!" (Genesis 1:31, emphasis added).

People marvel over sunrises, sunsets, and ocean views. People pay lots of money to go on safaris to stare at animals through binoculars. Those are all good, but God waited to call His creative work "very good" until after He made us!

What makes you "very good"? What makes you different from all the other amazing sights, sounds, and creatures God created? You were created in God's image, to be like Him. He did not make any other creature in His image. Only humanity.

He is relational, and He made you to relate to Him and others. He is creative, so you can be creative. He is wise, so you can grow in wisdom. He is loving, so you have the capacity to love. He is holy, and He invites His own to live holy.

Eden

Leaders, teachers, or parents sometimes use the phrase "made in the image of God" to encourage us when we're feeling down or struggling with self-doubt. It doesn't always help me in the moment because I often don't take the time to think about what it really means. Sometimes I assume it's like when people tell me, "Oh, you look just like your mom." But looking similar to my mom and being made in the image of the perfect God of the universe could not be more different. My mom didn't choose my features; she just got what she got when I was born! God created me in His perfect image, even though I am far from perfect.

I love my dog, Roscoe—the cutest goldendoodle you'll ever

meet. He never fails to make my friends laugh because he thinks everyone exists to give him belly rubs. I love him, but I did not create him. I couldn't have, even if I wanted to! But God's love for me is greater than my love for Roscoe. God had the power and desire to create me, and God had the power and desire to create you too. That's why you're here and reading this right now!

Not only did God create us, but He made us in His own image! The God of the universe chose us to be made in His likeness. Knowing He put His image on us helps me understand just how much He loves us and how special we are to Him. As great as Roscoe is, he wasn't made in God's image. But you and I and everyone we'll talk with today carries God's image in them.

The phrase "made in the image of God" challenges me in another way too. It's not just about how I see myself, but also how I see others. The phrase applies to every human being: the strict teacher, the girl who ignored me at school, the classmate who mocked my faith, and the guy I don't get along with. Because I am created in God's image, I can and should be kind and compassionate to others who are also made in His image. This truth can impact not just how I feel about myself but how I feel about others.

Reflection & Discussion Time

- What qualities do you have that are similar to qualities God has? For example, God is patient, and you might be patient too.
- When you remember that all people are created in the image of God, how does that change how you treat yourself and others?

God created human beings in his own image. In the image of God he created them; male and female he created them.

GENESIS 1:27

DAY 3

I Am Created with Intention

Eric

A growing number of teenagers express not feeling at home in their own bodies. Maybe you or a friend have felt this way: never fit in with the gender stereotypes of guys playing with toy trucks and rough sports or girls dressing up and playing with dolls, aren't happy and so badly want to be happy, and long for a sense of identity. TikTok features lots of videos about teenagers who have changed their gender identity, and they tell stories of being celebrated for their courage. Some think changing their gender could help them be known for something. Others struggle with a painful conflict within themselves, feeling as if their minds and bodies don't match—commonly called gender dysphoria. A film titled *Transgender Kids* puts it this way: "The heart of the debate about transgender kids is the idea your brain can be at war with your body."[1] This means the person's physical sex (how their body is designed) feels at war with their mind.

Do you know who else believes our minds and our bodies

can be at war with one another? Christians. We don't necessarily wrestle with our gender identity (though we may), but we wrestle internally with our sin and with living in a world that feels like a mismatch to who we are (see Romans 7:22-23). While God offers a solution different from changing our physical bodies, Christians can be compassionate because all of us, at some level, have not felt right in our own skin. So if you have a friend or family member who wrestles with gender dysphoria, you can and should be compassionate. If you experience this struggle personally, God is compassionate toward you, but He has a different path forward for you than the one the world offers.

The Creation account in the book of Genesis has a lot to say about gender. We see beautiful, intentionally designed distinctions in the way God created the world: day and night, land and sea, and male and female. Day and night come together to form our twenty-four-hour cycle. Land and sea come together to form the landscape of our world. Male and female come together, and God brings children from their union. We also see God and people come together. We are His creation, and He wants to be with us.

When God gave you your body, He decided whether you would be male or female. You may not love your body, but God designed you with great intention. If you struggle with a disconnect between your mind and your body, our culture says, *Listen to your mind and transform your body.* But is that wise? Think about how often our minds change. The Scripture says the opposite: *Offer your body to God and allow Him to transform your mind* (see Romans 12:1-2). Your body is a gift from Him. The way to be fulfilled is to see your body as a gift and offer yourself, including your body, to Him—to treat your body as ultimately belonging to God and to allow Him to continually work on your mind. Right now, He is doing just that! You are spending time with Him in Scripture, and He uses this time to form you.

Eden

Okay, I have to be honest: I was slow to learn all the terms used to describe gender and sexuality in our culture. When I was a freshman in high school, it was all very confusing with lots of new terms and acronyms being thrown around. Since then, I have learned that *gender* refers to how someone identifies and *sexuality* is about who someone is attracted to. I still get confused at times, but in conversations about gender, three things are more important to know than any new phrase or term you may see on social media.

First, God loves all people. He loves me, and He loves you. When discussions about gender and sexuality come up, it is important to remember we are talking about people He loves. All of us have our own struggles and challenges, but God's love does not stop because of these.

Second, God gave us our bodies. He made my body, and He made yours. When God created Adam, He created him as a man, and when He created Eve, God created Eve as a woman. Both were designed by God and are very valuable to Him. Just as day and night are different, so are guys and girls. There are amazing things about night and day—whether it's talking with friends at night under the stars or enjoying a sunny beach day. Both night and day are great in their own ways, but they are different from one another.

Third, we only find true fulfillment when we trust God's design. Going against His design, even if it feels right and good for a moment, always leads to pain. He is the Creator, the only non-created One, and we can trust His perfect design for us.

Reflection & Discussion Time

- What does it mean for a Christian to offer his or her body to God? How can you do that in your daily life?
- What are some things about your body that you're grateful for? List a few good things you can do with your body—for example, using your hands to write an encouraging note to a friend.

God blessed them and said, "Be fruitful and multiply. Fill the earth and govern it. Reign over the fish in the sea, the birds in the sky, and all the animals that scurry along the ground."

GENESIS 1:28

DAY 4

I Am Designed to Be Fruitful

Eric

Some people think being a Christian is only about the times you spend with God in prayer or at church. Not true! God designed you to make a difference in the world. Genesis 1:28 is famous for that reason and is often called "the cultural mandate" because God has designed you to be fruitful and to multiply in the culture. He has designed you to lead—to reign.

The Bible opens with humanity reigning under God's rule, and it ends with us reigning alongside Jesus, our eternal King (see Revelation 5:10). In the middle, in the here and now, we struggle and sin and often live like we are kings over our own lives instead of kings under His rule—which never works.

Those who read the verse about being fruitful and multiplying and only think about having kids miss some of the meaning. Yes, God loves when His followers bring kids into the world. But don't think you have to wait until you have kids one day to be fruitful and multiply. In fact, as you bring His love into the places where you go and as you help other people follow Jesus, you are being fruitful and multiplying.

- **At school, God wants you to be fruitful and multiply.** When you offer your schoolwork to Him by doing your best and using the mind He gave you, He does a great work in you and through you. Your teachers and classmates will notice your integrity and hard work, and God's Kingdom will multiply through you.
- **In sports or activities, God wants you to be fruitful and multiply.** When you offer your activities to Him, He will use you to encourage others. Your coaches and leaders will notice your joy, passion, and kindness to others, and they will see values of God's Kingdom in you.
- **In your life, God wants you to be fruitful and multiply.** Instead of using your gifts and blessings for yourself, use all you have received to serve others. As you serve others, you will be pointing people to the ultimate King.

God put Adam and Eve in the garden of Eden and commissioned them to reign and be fruitful. The garden was their domain. He has placed you in your school, in your neighborhood, on your team, and in your church. Be fruitful in all you do by knowing God has placed you there and by being a leader under Him, not trying to lead apart from Him.

Eden

When I think of being fruitful, I think of having babies. I'm pretty sure that's all I thought today's verse meant for a very long time.

Sure, God wants us to multiply physically, but this verse has a second meaning, which I love!

We are also called to "multiply" with our lives. He has called us to spread the gospel and pass God's love and grace to those around us. It's hard to believe we are entrusted with this great and amazing honor. We get to see people's lives changed for Jesus. I hope I never get over how awesome this is!

As a teenager, it can be scary to be bold and tell people about Jesus. There have been times when I was crippled by fear of judgment or just being thought of as weird. However, the gain of seeing Jesus move someone from death to life is worth it. If you have never shared your story with a friend, I want to encourage you to give it a try. Maybe share a time when Jesus was faithful to you. Think of it like this: Not sharing the gospel with someone is like knowing there's a fire and letting your friend sleep through it without waking them. There is so much power in the name of Jesus, and we have the opportunity to be salt and light to those around us. Whether we are at school, sports practice, rehearsals, or youth group, we should be fruitful and spread the gospel.

I have also seen Jesus multiply His great name when I serve at my church. I love kids with disabilities and get such great joy from serving with them. When we serve others and show them God's great love, we practice multiplication.

Reflection & Discussion Time

- How would you define the phrase "Be fruitful and multiply" for another teenager?
- What is one place in your life where you could be more fruitful as a Christian?

This High Priest of ours [Jesus] understands our weaknesses, for he faced all of the same testings we do, yet he did not sin.

HEBREWS 4:15

DAY 5

I Am a Tested Teenager like Jesus

Eric

Being a teenager has always been challenging. Lots of books have been written about the struggles of teenage life. Your body changes, your mind develops, and you have to make choices about your future. You face struggles with friends or fitting in, and you have to stay on top of schoolwork and other activities too.

We sometimes forget a very encouraging truth: Jesus was a teenager once. When He walked this earth, Jesus was fully God and fully human. He lived in a teenage body and faced all the teenage pressures you face. We have only a few verses in the Bible about Jesus as a teenager, but we know that He "was obedient to [his parents] . . . [and] grew in wisdom and in stature and in favor with God and all the people" (Luke 2:51-52). Jesus went through puberty and grew physically. Jesus learned in school and grew mentally. Jesus made friends in his neighborhood and grew in relationships with people.

Whatever age you are right now, Jesus has already lived that very age. Struggling with people disappointing you? Jesus knows what that is like. Feeling overwhelmed with everything? Jesus was overwhelmed too. Whatever pressure you are facing, Jesus has faced that pressure. If you had a great day, Jesus knows that feeling. If you had a horrible day, Jesus knows that feeling too.

He faced all the same testing you do, yet He did not sin. He can understand you because He knows exactly what it is like to be a teenager. But He can also help you because He is God and did not sin (see Hebrews 4:15). There is no one like Jesus! No one but Jesus fully gets you and is perfect at the same time.

When you pray to Jesus, He knows you and understands you. He loves when you go to Him in prayer, and He is able to give you wisdom, comfort, and strength. Knowing that Jesus understands you should inspire you to "come boldly to the throne of our gracious God. There we will receive his mercy, and we will find grace to help us when we need it most" (Hebrews 4:16).

Eden

Transitioning from a kid to an adult is what we call *adolescence*, and it can be pretty weird and awkward. Now that I'm a junior in high school, I look so different from how I looked as a freshman. Things change a lot, and they change fast.

It's a bit weird at first to think of the Jesus I worship and follow being a teenager. However, when I do, it's actually really comforting. I've heard adults say they wish they could have skipped the horrible teenage years. That has always bothered me because, come on, teenage years can't be all bad, right? Jesus could have easily chosen to skip the teenage years himself, but He didn't. Being fully God and fully man, He chose to experience all the teenage emotions. He had moments of sadness, He experienced emotional hurt, and I bet He even had friendship issues. Knowing that He went through these years so He could relate to me makes me remember how much He loves me.

Do you ever feel like no one understands you? Jesus does! Not only does He understand us, but He knows our innermost thoughts and feelings. The ones that no one else knows. The ones that hurt too much to say aloud. He knows them, understands them, and has great compassion on us. When I'm going through tough times, I do my best to remember that He understands because He experienced pain too. He experienced the worst kind of pain—the weight of all of my sin on the cross. He was thinking about us in that moment too!

Knowing that Jesus understands what it's like to be a teenager is really inspiring too. Even though we are not perfect, we can still serve and impact others as Jesus did. We are not too young to be used by Him! I am currently seeing this to be true in my life. Along with a team of others, I help lead a Friday-night Bible study for juniors and seniors who want to go deeper in their faith. It's amazing to see what God is doing in our lives as we lead, but also in the lives of the teenagers who come every week. I am truly in awe that He is using me because I am so far from having it all together—but I am so thankful.

Reflection & Discussion Time

- If Jesus were a teenager today who went to your school, what would He be like? Who would He hang out with?
- Jesus can relate to everything you're going through—He experienced life as a teenager too! How could that change how you think about communicating with Him through prayer?

God saved you by his grace when you believed. And you can't take credit for this; it is a gift from God. Salvation is not a reward for the good things we have done, so none of us can boast about it. For we are God's masterpiece. He has created us anew in Christ Jesus, so we can do the good things he planned for us long ago.

EPHESIANS 2:8-10

DAY 6

I Am His Masterpiece

Eric

You may not know this, but the New Testament in your Bible was originally written in Greek and then translated into other languages, including English. You don't need to know Greek to read and understand the Bible, but sometimes there is a really cool meaning in the original Greek language that helps you appreciate a verse more. This is one of those times. The word for "masterpiece" in Ephesians 2:10 is *poiema*. It is the word we get the English word *poem* from. In other words, you are God's artwork, His poem, His handiwork.

Think about something you created that you were very proud of—maybe something from art, music, creative writing, or shop class. If you loved what you created, you were likely very protective of your masterpiece. An artist never wants someone to harm or speak negatively of their work, but to savor and appreciate it.

All the art we create falls short of God's masterpieces because, well, He is God and we are not. And you are His masterpiece.

He created you in your mother's womb, and when you believed in Him, He created you anew. Jesus even taught that we are "born again" when we believe in Him (see John 3:3)—that we get a brand-new life, a brand-new identity. He saved you by His grace, not by the good things you have done. But because you are His masterpiece, He has good things planned for you to do. Long ago, God planned the good things you would do for Him as you serve others in this world.

God has given you your personality, abilities, gifts, and passions, and now that He has made you new—made you His child by His grace—He plans to equip you to show others that He loves them too.

Eden

I am God's masterpiece. This is really hard for me to believe most days when what I really feel like is a mess. I have a bit (a lot) of a perfectionist spirit. My mom would disagree with this when it comes to my room at times, but it is very true when it comes to both academics and athletics. Imagine how much of a failure I felt like in elementary school when I struggled to learn to read and spell. As a young elementary student, I could not have disliked school more. I did well and scored high on tests, but it was *hard.* When I was diagnosed with dyslexia in third grade, I was so relieved to know my struggle had a name. I remember a reading specialist telling me, "Eden, nothing is wrong with you. Your brain just works differently. You have the ability to think in a much different way than others. Dyslexia is a gift." This one conversation shifted my perspective. My brain wasn't a mess; it was a masterpiece. Jesus made me like this, and He would use it for His purposes. I didn't fully understand this at the time, but as a junior attending a liberal arts high school and participating in AP and honors courses, I now see the reading specialist was right. I have been able to encourage other kids who are struggling because I truly believe God has used dyslexia to make me better in so many ways. But more than that, He has used my "different" brain to show me Himself and how much He loves me. He has answered prayer after prayer when it comes to academic success, and I now *love* school and learning. What I once thought was a mess is clearly a masterpiece for Him.

Ephesians 2:8-10 not only tells me that I am God's masterpiece—every part of me—but that He saved me and gave me a new heart so I can do the good things He planned for me long ago. When I worry about my future, and basically have no clue what will happen, it's comforting to remember that Jesus sees my future so clearly. He made me, He saved me, and He sets my future before me. Wow, what a great God.

Reflection & Discussion Time

- What are some abilities or gifts God has given you?
- What are some good works you could do with those abilities or gifts?

Don't you realize that your body is the temple of the Holy Spirit, who lives in you and was given to you by God? You do not belong to yourself, for God bought you with a high price. So you must honor God with your body.

1 CORINTHIANS 6:19-20

DAY 7

I Am Where God Lives

Eric

When Eden got her license, we let her drive my old Jeep Wrangler. At least I thought she was just going to be driving it. But she kinda moved in. She put some rubber duckies in the Jeep because evidently that is a thing now. She threw some blankets in the back so when she goes to the beach with her friends, she is ready. She stuck her sunglasses in the compartment and took mine out. She was not content just to drive the Jeep; she needed to make it her own, to change some things.

When you became a Christian, God the Spirit moved into your life. Your body is the temple of the Holy Spirit. In the Old Testament, the temple was the place where God would meet with people. When Jesus entered our world, He referred to Himself as the temple (see John 2:13-19) because He is "God with us." Jesus called Himself the temple and did things that were typically done in the temple. He received worship from people. He pronounced forgiveness to people when they thought they had to go to the temple and offer a sacrifice to be forgiven. So instead of requiring people to go to a temple to meet with God, Jesus came as the temple. Now *you* are the temple! God lives within you. This is mind-blowing, I know.

We bought the Jeep we have with money, but God bought you with the blood of Jesus. You no longer belong to yourself, but to Him. Just like Eden was not content just to be in the Jeep, God is not content just to live within you. He wants to completely redecorate you. He wants to direct you, to steer your whole life. This is always good for you.

This week you have seen how valuable you are and how valuable your body is. God created you in His image, knit you together, designed you, called you His masterpiece, and moved into your life.

"So you must honor God with your body."

Eden

When I was in preschool, my mom took my sister and me with her to a Bible study that had a kids' program. One song I still remember was about "the gift of the Holy Spirit." I remember part of the song went, "The Holy Spirit is the third person of the Trinity who comes to live in me." As a four-year-old, I didn't fully understand it, but I knew three things: First, He's a gift, and I like gifts! Second, He is God. Third, He lives in me.

As I have gotten older, the reality of this has become so much heavier and almost overwhelmingly amazing. God lives in me? Think about that for a second. The God who created the universe and hung the stars in the sky lives in you. That means I have access to all of His goodness, His kindness, His wisdom, everything. He is there when I am lonely and scared, when I feel like a failure or inadequate. So why do I forget to go to Him first? Why do I forget He has the best advice and can guide every step? I think it's because I get too caught up in my own world and my own desires.

A verse that comes to mind is James 4:5, which says, "Do you think it's without reason that the Scripture says: The spirit he made to dwell in us envies intensely?" (CSB). He is jealous for me. He wants all of me! He loves me so much that He won't let anything take up the place where only He belongs. When we wrestle with things in our life that compete with space the Holy Spirit should have, we might as well give them to Him because He's going to win. I have learned (and I'm still learning) that it can be a long battle or a short one—that's up to me.

Reflection & Discussion Time

- What does it mean to dishonor God with our bodies? What can you do to resist the temptation to do this?
- Are there any changes you need to make in your life to better honor God with your body?

Memory Verse

See what great love the Father has given us that we should be called God's children—and we are!

1 JOHN 3:1, CSB

WEEK TWO

God Loved Me First

To all who believed him and accepted him, he gave the right to become children of God. They are reborn—not with a physical birth resulting from human passion or plan, but a birth that comes from God.

JOHN 1:12-13

DAY 8

I Am Reborn

Eric

Have you ever heard someone say, "We are all God's children"? It is true that God created and loves every single person, but according to the Scripture, you must be reborn to become God's child. Our sin—our failure to live as we should—separated us all from God, and believing in Jesus is the only way we are brought into a close relationship with God—a relationship so close we become His children. When you believed in Jesus and received Him as your Savior and Lord, He gave you the right to become His child. It was not a rebirth you could make happen because you could not forgive yourself or make yourself brand new. It was a rebirth God accomplished for you. When you believed in Him, He made you forever His.

You are now God's son or daughter. He is your Father.

If you have a great earthly father, this is probably easier to understand. If you don't have an earthly father or your earthly dad is absent, the concept of God as your Father may be harder to understand.

Author Warren Farrell coined the phrase "dad deprivation" about the pain some teenagers go through when their father is absent.[1] The pain is common. If you have not been well-loved by an earthly dad, I am sorry. If you suffer the pain of being deprived of an earthly father, God promises to step in close. Psalm 68:5 (CSB) says: "God in his holy dwelling is a father of the fatherless and a champion of widows." Because you now belong to Him, you are no longer fatherless.

Whether you have a good earthly father or not, your heavenly Father is never going to let you down. He is with you. He is never going to walk out. He is never going to take on too much responsibility at work and neglect you for a season. He is never going to be too busy for you. He is never going to stop providing for you. He is never going to change His mind about you. He is never going to just send Christmas gifts and fail to show up and actually be with you.

Eden

In the last decade both of my parents have lost their dads. As a teen, it's a normal thing to go through the loss of a grandparent. For me, watching my parents grieve over their fathers' deaths was hard. They both had such special relationships with their dads. Dads have a huge impact on our lives. When I was little, I would try so hard to impress my dad with how I performed. Whether it was a swim meet, a spelling test, or how I could do more push-ups than the boys, I wanted to make my dad proud. I am one of the lucky ones, because I have a *great* dad. He has shown my sister and me Jesus' love in the ways he has loved us.

If you don't have a good dad or he is absent from your life, I am so sorry. But I have great news! Just as much as a father figure impacts us as teens, God is an even greater Father whose love impacts us even more. My dad says, "God is not the reflection of your earthly father, but the perfection of your earthly father." Earthly fathers are good and sometimes even great, but God the Father is perfect. When we receive Jesus into our lives, we are reborn as His children. There couldn't be a better Father. He chooses us, loves us, forgives us, protects us, and is always with us. As a teen, parents are so vital for our growth and well-being. Dads are especially important. Our earthly dads and father figures are reflections of our heavenly Father's love for us. As teens, we need our dads in our lives, and we need our heavenly Father even more!

Reflection & Discussion Time

- What characteristics do teenagers long for in an earthly father? How do you see those characteristics in your heavenly Father?
- What would change about tomorrow if you remembered throughout the day that God is your Father?

See what great love the Father has given us that we should be called God's children—and we are!

1 JOHN 3:1, CSB

DAY 9

I Am Actually His Child

Eric

I want you to respond to some questions today's verse that I think will help you understand who God is and who you are. Go ahead and write down the answers to these questions:

- How much does God love you?

- How did you get His love?

- Whose child are you?

- Are you only *called* His child?

God has given you His great love. His love is greater than any human love. He has loved you more than anyone ever has or ever will.

You did not earn or pay for His love. He gave you His love and set His affection on you. He loved you first, before you ever thought of loving Him. He expressed His love by dying for you on the cross to take away your sin and make you His child.

You are not merely called His child; you *actually are* His child! We all know people who have been called things that are not true. Or people who have pretended to be someone they are not. But that's not the case for God's children!

God is the eternal King, and you are His son or daughter. Like other famous people, human kings are hard to get to—and almost impossible to sit down with and talk to. They have bodyguards and busy schedules and long lines of people who would love to just get a picture with them. Most people will never speak to a human king. But one person can always get the attention of a good king: the king's child. Congratulations—the everlasting King is also your Dad! You can approach Him at any time. In fact, when Jesus taught His disciples to pray, He told them to pray, "Our Father" (Matthew 6:9). Jesus wants you to remember that God is your Father.

Eden

I think we all know it's not fun to be called names that don't fully represent us or that put us in a box. One name I am called semiregularly is "pastor's kid." This is an accurate name for me because my dad is a pastor, and I am his child. I actually love being a pastor's kid! However, I don't like the name when it is used to accuse me of things that are not true, such as "You only got to do so and so because your dad is the pastor" or "I heard all pastors' kids are secretly bad." What? I have worked hard for my accomplishments and because Jesus gave me a new heart and His Spirit, I'm not bad! So as much as I love being my dad's child, the term "pastor's kid" isn't always used to describe me correctly.

Many concepts in the Bible can be confusing, but this statement is so clear and amazing: We are God's children! When God calls you His child, He actually means it. And it's not just a title—we also get the privileges that come with it. We are able to talk to the King of the universe whenever we want because the King is also our Dad! We get His care and protection. We are His heirs—meaning He will give us an everlasting and stunning inheritance one day in heaven. Being called His child is *not* like that participation trophy our soccer coach gave us or the pity character award we got from our teacher. Sure, those were nice, but this is different and better. It's real!

Reflection & Discussion Time

- What titles have you been most proud of in your life? Why is being called God's child even better?
- Why is it important to understand that God loves you because you are His child—not because of anything you've done?

God decided in advance to adopt us into his own family by bringing us to himself through Jesus Christ. This is what he wanted to do, and it gave him great pleasure.

EPHESIANS 1:5

DAY 10

I Am Adopted by God

Eric

When a friend of mine was in junior high school, a classmate made fun of him for being adopted. My friend went home from school upset, and his mom could tell he was hurt. After she asked him over and over again what was wrong, my friend finally told her about the mean kid and what he said.

His mom told him, "If he does it again, tell him that his parents got stuck with him, but we chose you. We picked you!"

When a child is adopted, he or she does not have to audition to be in the family—the family goes to great lengths to bring the child home. When a child is adopted, the child does not pursue the parents—the parents pursue the child. There are no accidental adoptions. The parents decide to adopt and pursue the child, and they are thrilled to bring him or her home.

Not only are you God's child, but a theme throughout Scripture is that you are God's *adopted* child. Notice that today's verse teaches that God decided in advance to adopt you. He wanted you. He was not surprised when you became His. He is the One who took the initiative, and it gave Him great pleasure that you became His child.

Notice how you became His child, how you were brought into His family. He brought you to Himself "through Jesus Christ." God is perfect, and you are not. So He came to earth as a human—Jesus—and took your sin and shame from you on the cross. The cross was planned just as your adoption into God's family was planned.

While Jesus prayed to the Father and taught us to pray "Our Father," there is one time in the Gospels where Jesus does not address God as Father. When Jesus was on the cross, He yelled out a verse from an Old Testament psalm: "My God, My God, why have you forsaken me?" (Matthew 27:46, ESV). In that moment, Jesus endured the punishment for our sin so there would only be grace for us who believe. Jesus experienced the feeling of separation from the Father so you would never be separated. Jesus suffered so you could be adopted!

Eden

I remember the day we adopted my dog, Roscoe. I'd wanted a dog for the longest time. I begged and begged my parents. I even did research and created a slideshow for my parents on why we should get a dog and then an additional slideshow on why a mini goldendoodle would be the perfect choice. They seemed to have a lot of excuses for not getting a dog! When we moved to California, though, they caved, and we got Roscoe. I still take pride in picking Roscoe. There is no better dog, and everyone knows it.

While a pet of any kind cannot remotely compare to humans

who are made in the image of God, we can see a parallel when it comes to being adopted. If you have ever adopted a pet like I have, you may have done a lot of research to make sure you were choosing the right pet. No one wants a dog who bites little kids and constantly pees on the floor. God, however, doesn't have to research us at all because He created us and knows our innermost thoughts and plans and still chooses to adopt us and make us His own! This blows my mind because I'm pretty sure I would not have chosen myself before I was His or even on most days now.

It's one thing to be someone's child, and it is another to be chosen as their child. The more I think about it, the more I realize how incredible the love of adoptive parents is. Consider how much more God loves His children! Not only does He choose us, but God sent His Son, Jesus, to die on the cross for us so we could be brought home to Him. It is comforting to know that God is our loving Father.

Reflection & Discussion Time

- What have you wanted to be chosen for as a teenager? How is being chosen to be God's child even better?
- How does it make you feel that God adopted you? How could it impact the way you relate to others?

That is why I tell you not to worry about everyday life—whether you have enough food and drink, or enough clothes to wear. Isn't life more than food, and your body more than clothing? Look at the birds. They don't plant or harvest or store food in barns, for your heavenly Father feeds them. And aren't you far more valuable to him than they are? Can all your worries add a single moment to your life?

And why worry about your clothing? Look at the lilies of the field and how they grow. They don't work or make their clothing, yet Solomon in all his glory was not dressed as beautifully as they are. And if God cares so wonderfully for wildflowers that are here today and thrown into the fire tomorrow, he will certainly care for you. Why do you have so little faith?

So don't worry about these things, saying, "What will we eat? What will we drink? What will we wear?" These things dominate the thoughts of unbelievers, but your heavenly Father already knows all your needs. Seek the Kingdom of God above all else, and live righteously, and he will give you everything you need.

So don't worry about tomorrow, for tomorrow will bring its own worries. Today's trouble is enough for today.

MATTHEW 6:25-34

DAY 11

I Am Filled with Wonder

Eric

Grab a pen and underline every *worry* and *Father* you see in today's passage.

Jesus was teaching a crowd to not worry, but He did not merely say "Don't worry" because He knew that would not help. What does help is replacing our worry with wonder, so Jesus pointed to the wonder of being cared for by our heavenly Father. God, our Father, is perfect and loving—and He takes care of the wildflowers, so He will take care of you because you matter much more to Him.

More worry typically means less wonder.

More wonder typically means less worry.

It's not possible to be filled with both wonder and worry at the same time. You can wonder or you can worry, but you can't do both. Spending a lot of time on social media likely increases your worry, but what increases your wonder? For me, a long bike ride looking at God's creation increases my awe. Reading a book about Him, reflecting on Scripture, waiting in the ocean for a wave as the sun rises—all those moments help increase my wonder. To decrease your worry, increase your wonder for your Father—your wonder that God has made you His child.

Eden

We have been called "the anxious generation" because a bunch of research shows we struggle with anxiety more than previous generations.[1] Because of social media, we even have new terms like FOMO. Even before I was a teenager, I struggled with worry a lot, and becoming a teenager seemed to make the worry worse. I found myself worrying about sports, school, public speaking, the future, and even worrying itself. I would worry about when I would worry next!

I saw a counselor. I talked to my parents. I took medicine. All of that has helped, but what has helped me the most is spending time with Jesus in His Word. Yes, I still get anxious, but now I know how to handle it better because when I start to worry, I can remind myself how good my heavenly Father is and that He has the best intentions for me! The more I experience wonder for Him, the less worry I tend to have. Listening to worship music, talking with friends about God around a firepit, and reading my Bible all increase my wonder.

Next time you get anxious, remember that your God is a loving Father who never leaves you. Even if you embarrass yourself, fail your test, or don't make the team, He is still there and still good.

Reflection & Discussion Time

- What increases worry in your life?
- What increases wonder for God as your Father?
- What changes could you make in your life to decrease worry and increase wonder?

You have not received a spirit that makes you fearful slaves. Instead, you received God's Spirit when he adopted you as his own children. Now we call him, "Abba, Father." For his Spirit joins with our spirit to affirm that we are God's children. And since we are his children, we are his heirs.

ROMANS 8:15-17

DAY 12

I Am Not a Slave to Fear

Eric

For four years I led a group of high school guys in a Bible study—from their freshman year in high school until they graduated. Each time we gathered, we would share burdens and concerns so we could pray for one another. You won't be surprised to hear that a common request for prayer was about fear. Afraid of not doing well on a big, looming test. Afraid of the pressure at a big game. Afraid of making the wrong decision about college. Afraid of asking a girl on a date because she might say no. And the list goes on. Fear can make you a slave. It can boss you around, steal your joy, and fill your mind with worry.

What are three things you are afraid of at times?

1. ....

2. ....

3. ....

While you may struggle with fear, if you are a Christian, you are not a *slave* to fear. Fear no longer runs your life if you have received God's Spirit because God's Spirit is stronger than a spirit of fear.

Based on today's verses, let me break down for you the awesome news of what happened to you when you believed in Jesus. The moment you believed, you were adopted as God's child. God sent His Holy Spirit into your life, and His Spirit constantly reminds your spirit that you are God's child. He has not delegated that to an angel or to someone else. God Himself reminds you to relate to Him as Father. You now can call God "Abba, Father."

"Abba" was the word children in Bible times used when they were very young as a sign of affection for their fathers. God, whom some view as distant and unknowable, is your Father! Because this passage is from the book of Romans, we know it was first written to people living in Rome. At this time, a third of the Roman Empire were slaves. Slaves often lived in fear of their masters and had no possessions of their own. This is not true of you. You have been adopted and are even an heir of Christ—meaning you will enjoy life forever with Him.

Eden

Fear is one of the biggest obstacles that holds me back from opportunities, trying new things, and putting myself out there. The three things I'm most likely to be afraid of are:

1. What others think of me and my reputation
2. Not being good enough or achieving enough
3. Being lonely and not loved

For many teens, including me, fear is a big obstacle to overcome. It feels like there is so much pressure on our generation. With the demands of social media, school, and sports, life can feel overwhelming, and fear can quickly rise. It can even feel like we are slaves to fear, as it can take hold of our emotions, thoughts, and actions.

Although it can feel like fear has us in chains, this is not true. We are not slaves to fear if we are children of God. We don't need to feel captive to fear because we can rest in Him. When we get fearful about our biology test, we can rest. When we get fearful about our sports game, we can rest. And when we get fearful about friend drama, we can rest. Of course, this is easier said than done. My parents have told me many times not to worry, but sometimes I don't know how to control that feeling! We may wrestle with fear, but we can choose to bring our fear to our Father.

Reflection & Discussion Time

- Why do you think many people view God as distant and not as Father?
- How would seeing God as your Father help you with your fears?

Trust in the L*ORD* *with all your heart;*
do not depend on your own understanding.
Seek his will in all you do,
and he will show you which path to take.

PROVERBS 3:5-6

DAY 13

I Am a Child of a Trustworthy Father

Eric

Have you ever seen a little kid at a swimming pool, standing on the edge with her dad in the water saying, "Come on, jump! You can trust me. I got you!" The kid is nervous but finally jumps, and the dad loves it because the kid is honoring the dad by trusting him. In the same way, your heavenly Father is honored when you trust Him.

While we are all tempted to trust in ourselves, deep down we know we are not the most trustworthy. We break promises to ourselves. We don't live up to our own standards. We are not all-powerful and wise, not like our heavenly Father. While He loves when we trust Him, it is also good for us to trust Him. Don't depend on your own understanding or strength. Instead, jump to Him, and depend on Him.

On the next page are some verses that give you reasons you can trust God, who is the perfect Father. Read them aloud and mark the ones that mean the most to you at this time in your life.

- **Loving:** "See what great love the Father has given us that we should be called God's children—and we are!" (1 John 3:1, CSB).

- **Generous and consistent:** "Every good and perfect gift is from above, coming down from the Father of lights, who does not change like shifting shadows" (James 1:17, CSB).

- **Compassionate:** "As a father has compassion on his children, so the LORD has compassion on those who fear him" (Psalm 103:13, CSB).

- **Sovereign:** "Aren't two sparrows sold for a penny? Yet not one of them falls to the ground without your Father's consent" (Matthew 10:29, CSB).

- **Powerful:** "My Father, who has given them to me, is greater than all. No one is able to snatch them out of the Father's hand" (John 10:29, CSB).

Eden

You know how when we were little, we would do "trust falls"? In a trust fall, you fall back and trust that the person standing behind you is going to catch you. It was all fun and games until someone got dropped! After that, no one wanted to be the next trust-fall victim.

Just as we tried to trust our friends or classmates to catch us, we need to trust that our heavenly Father will catch us. I know that's a little different (okay, a lot different) because unlike our friends,

God will never fail to catch us. Even when it feels like we are close to the ground, He is still there. We don't need to worry whether He will be good to us, because He has never failed. Goodness is part of His character. It's who He is!

From my dad's list of reasons we can trust God, "powerful" provides the most comfort to me. My Father is greater than all my fears, greater than all my problems, and greater than my shame. He is more than powerful enough to protect me. He's my all-powerful bodyguard. Whenever I'm having a hard time trusting my Father, I will remind myself that He holds all the power. Next time you're not sure you can trust God, remind yourself of all His trustworthy characteristics.

Reflection & Discussion Time

- Why do the verses that you marked above mean the most to you?
- What is something you are struggling to trust God with? How could reminding yourself of His character help you?

Imitate God, therefore, in everything you do,
because you are his dear children.

EPHESIANS 5:1

DAY 14

I Am a Child of a Father I Want to Imitate

Eric

When my daughters were small and I tucked them into bed, we had the same routine every night. I would ask them, "Does Daddy love you because you are pretty?"

I taught them to say, "No."

"You are pretty, but Daddy does not love you because of that. Does Daddy love you because you are smart?"

"No."

"You are smart, but that is not why Daddy loves you. Does Daddy love you because you obey?"

"No."

"I am grateful when you obey your parents, but that is not why I love you. Why does Daddy love you?"

And I taught them to say, "Daddy loves me because he loves me."

I wanted them to know that my love for them is not based on their performance but based on our relationship. I also wanted them to know that God's love for them works the same way. He loves you because He loves you. Not because of anything you have done. When you get this—when you understand His love for you is fixed—it does not cause you to run from God so you can "get away with something" but to run *to* Him. Don't you want to run to a heavenly Father like that?

God invites you to obey Him not so He will love you but because He already does. God commands you to imitate Him not so you can become His child but because you already are. Here are some passages where He invites you to imitate Him because you are His:

- Be merciful as He is merciful (see Luke 6:36, CSB).
- Be humble because He humbled Himself (see Philippians 2:7-8).
- Be compassionate as He is compassionate (see Ephesians 4:32, CSB).
- Be holy as He is holy (see 1 Peter 1:16).
- Be generous as He is generous (see 2 Corinthians 8:9).
- Be forgiving as He forgave you (Colossians 3:13).

He loves you because He loves you, and because you have experienced His love, imitate Him!

Eden

I remember how my dad tucked me in every night and said those words. He also sang me a song with these lyrics: "Oh, He loves you, oh, He loves you, just because He does." Those words stuck with me all through my childhood until now. My dad imitated God's love for me. When he said those words, my dad reminded me of the Father's unconditional love for me.

Just like my dad imitates God as a father, there are plenty of people we teens want to imitate. Maybe for you it's a famous athlete, an actor, a friend or a classmate, or even a mentor or a parent. These people have qualities or skills that draw us to imitate them.

While it's not wrong to look up to celebrities or people in our lives, the person we should most focus on imitating is Jesus. He lived a perfect life in a sinful world, and He is the ultimate role model. As much as we want to be like those other people we look up to, how much more should we want to imitate Jesus?! Not only is He perfect, but He loved us first. It is His unconditional love that leads us to love others.

Out of all the attributes in the list above, I want to work on practicing humility the most. At our age, it's hard not to want to talk about our achievements or try to assert ourselves. But the biggest thing to remember is this: I can be humble because Jesus humbled Himself first. He's so humble that He was willing to die a shameful death in our place. You may choose another one of your heavenly Father's attributes to focus on. I need help on lots of them, to be honest!

Reflection & Discussion Time

- Look at the list of verses on the previous page, which challenge you to imitate God. Which one comes most naturally to you? Which one do you need Him to help you with the most?
- Why do you think the Bible tells us to imitate our heavenly Father?

Memory Verse

Since we have been justified through faith, we have peace with God through our Lord Jesus Christ.

ROMANS 5:1, CSB

WEEK THREE

God Has Made Me Right with Himself

Since we have been justified through faith, we have peace with God through our Lord Jesus Christ.

ROMANS 5:1, CSB

DAY 15

I Am "Just as If I Never Sinned"

Eric

One of the first trades someone made with Bitcoin is an unbelievable story. Laszlo Hanyecz was working his computer programming job, and he was hungry. Bitcoin was not worth any money at the time, but Laszlo posted online that he would pay with Bitcoin for two pizzas. Someone came to his place with two pizzas from Papa John's, and he gave the person 10,000 Bitcoins. As we write this, that is worth 600 million dollars. Laszlo traded 600 million dollars for two pizzas!

Jesus made an even more amazing trade. When He died willingly on the cross, He took all your sin upon Himself. He traded your sin for His righteousness. Thanks to Jesus' death and resurrection, you are now justified.

Justified isn't a common word, but it's a very important word. In the Bible, *justified* describes what God did for you when you placed your faith in Christ. A common and helpful way to remember what *justified* means is this:

Justified = Just-as-if-I never sinned

Because those of us who believe in Jesus have been justified, we now have peace with God. Instead of being at war with Him, we have confidence that He is for us. We did not always have peace with God. All of us have disobeyed God, rebelled against Him, and made ourselves His enemy. It's not possible to find peace with God on our own—He had to make peace with us. He did just that "through our Lord Jesus Christ." Some people miss out on Jesus by thinking they are too bad, they have done too many things wrong, or that God would never want to be at peace with them. Not true. He is eager to welcome them into His family, and Jesus came to our world to make that possible. Some miss out on Jesus by thinking they are too good—that they don't need Him. But all of us need to be justified to have peace with God.

You have been justified. It is just as if you never lied, never disobeyed your parents, never cheated, never lost your temper, never gossiped, never envied, never did anything wrong. God looks at you as if you have never once sinned! God sees you as perfect, not because you are, but because Jesus is, and Jesus has covered you. So you don't need to live with shame because Christ put your shame to shame on the cross.

Eden

I hate to admit it, but I have made a couple driving mistakes. I got my license in December of 2023, when I had only been sixteen for two months. I was so excited to be able to drive myself to school, go wherever I wanted whenever I wanted (that didn't actually happen!), and blast music in the car. It was a little scary for the first few days, but the taste of freedom helped me get over my fear pretty fast. I hit a few things in those first weeks, but no people. W for me! However, parking was not my specialty. One time, after leaving a birthday party, I hit a garage door. In my defense, it was in a very tight and dark alley. I called my parents, took a photo of the door, and left a note with my phone number.

Crazy enough, the lady called me, said she was grateful I left a note, and forgave me! She didn't make me pay for anything. I was soooo grateful that I could save this money! I did not deserve the grace she showed toward me. She treated me as if I'd never messed up—never hit the garage—and my penalty was erased.

Jesus does this for us too, but on a much greater scale. We are justified—treated as if we have never sinned. He took on all our sin when He died on the cross. We are made clean and forgiven. As teens, it's such a relief to know Jesus looks at us as if we have never sinned or made one mistake.

The teen years are hard—trust me, I know it well. Because I am in them! There is a lot going on with school, sports, family, friends, relationships, and so much more. It's hard to navigate life through these years. And we are not going to do it perfectly. We might talk back to our parents, make some mistakes with friends, fail a test, and maybe even hit a garage. But no matter what, Jesus will forgive us when we turn to Him. He covers our sins and washes us white as snow.

Reflection & Discussion Time

- How would you explain the word *justified* to a friend?
- Think of a time someone forgave you for something you did wrong. How did you feel?

God has united you with Christ Jesus. For our benefit God made him to be wisdom itself. Christ made us right with God; he made us pure and holy, and he freed us from sin.

1 CORINTHIANS 1:30

DAY 16

I am "Just as If I Always Obeyed"

Eric

Yesterday we talked about the beauty of being justified ("just-as-if-I never sinned"). That's an amazing and beautiful truth but also only half of what it means to be justified. There is even more!

Justified = Just-as-if-I always obeyed

Not only did Jesus remove all your sin, but He also gave you all of His righteousness. Not only did He forgive the debt of what you owe; He filled your account with all His holiness and purity.

I was teaching at a youth camp one summer about being justified, and a young man came up to me after the message. He asked, "So are you saying it's like Jesus erased all the bad grades on my report card and put His perfect grades in their place?" "You just explained it perfectly," I said. "That is exactly what Jesus did for you when you believed in Him."

Many believe that Michael Jordan's greatest basketball game

happened against the Cavaliers in 1990 when he scored 69 points in an overtime win. On his team was a rookie named Stacey King who struggled and only scored one point. After the game was over, Jordan rushed to the locker room, and the reporters decided to talk to King since Jordan was nowhere to be found. King said to the reporters, "I'll always remember this as the night that Michael Jordan and I combined to score 70 points."[1]

Stacey King was wise to attach himself to Jordan's performance. And we are wise if we attach ourselves to Jesus because all of Jesus' righteousness gets credited to our account. We do not even bring one point to the table, though. All we brought was our sin, and Jesus took that from us!

You are justified. God looks at you just as if you always told the truth, obeyed your parents, lived with integrity, practiced patience, and used your tongue to encourage others. Of course, none of us have lived perfectly on our own, but if you are united with Jesus, that is how God sees you!

Eden

When I was little, I had a friend whose parents gave him a sticker chart. The sticker chart was a piece of paper on the fridge. Every time my friend did something good, he got a sticker. Because of the sticker chart, he obeyed extra well. Once the chart was full of stickers, he was able to pick out a toy. I really wanted one of those sticker charts. So my dad finally got me one.

The problem was, I only obeyed to get a sticker. It was not out of the goodness of my heart or because I loved my parents. Eventually, my dad recognized this and decided to teach me a lesson. One day I came into the kitchen, and my sticker chart was full!

"Eden, do you know who filled the sticker chart?" Dad said.

"Did Daddy?"

"Yes," my dad said. "This is how much Jesus loves you. He gives you rewards you don't deserve. You are treated as if you are always obedient. He fills your sticker chart because you would never be able to do it on your own!"

Of course, I still wanted my toy—and my dad took me to get it even though I had not earned it myself. (It was an Ariel doll, in case you were wondering.)

Jesus has filled our sticker charts! He gives us His righteousness, so we look to Him as if we have always obeyed. He takes every messy mistake that we make as teens, and He not only erases them but looks at us as if we are perfect and flawless children. In His eyes, we didn't slip that bad word or treat our siblings poorly. No. He took all of our sins and replaced them with His goodness. We don't have to live in shame or fear. We can rest knowing He has transformed us by His grace.

Reflection & Discussion Time

- Why do you think Stacey King combined his score with Michael Jordan's? What could it look like for you to "attach yourself" to Jesus in this way?
- How do you think your life would change if you truly believed that God has filled up your sticker chart even though you don't deserve it?

To those who are the called, loved by God the Father and kept for Jesus Christ.

JUDE 1:1, CSB

DAY 17

I Am Kept

Eric

"You got this." Friends sometimes use that phrase to encourage us and help us feel confident. It typically comes from a good place, but sometimes it can feel untrue. When I went mountain biking for the first time, a friend told me, "You got this, Eric." And I thought, *No, technically I don't. I have no idea what I am doing!*

Then there are times when people tell us, "I got you." If we don't always believe *we've* "got this," why would we believe someone else has us? If you have been damaged by someone who once said, "I got you," it is even more difficult to believe. If you live with the pain of being let down or being betrayed like this, it can be hard to trust again.

Some people view living as a Christian as God telling us, "You got this. You can do this!" But that view only increases our worry and insecurity because deep down we know we still struggle. Instead, God wants you to view life as a Christian as Him reminding you, "I got this. I got you." Unlike others who have let you down or betrayed you, God never does. He called you to Himself. He loved you first. And He keeps you for and to Himself.

You are kept! Meaning you will always be His child because He will always keep you as His child.

Jesus described His ability to keep you: "My sheep listen to my voice; I know them, and they follow me. I give them eternal life, and they will never perish. No one can snatch them away from me" (John 10:27-28). No one can take you from Jesus or take away the eternal life He has given to you. You are kept not by your ability to hold on to Him but by His promise to hold on to you. You are kept not by your goodness but by His grace, not by your strength but by His. No one can snatch you out of His hand, and He will never discard you. He paid for you with His own blood on the cross, so there is no way He is giving you up. You are His treasured possession, and He holds you tight.

Wherever you go today—school, work, church, home—know that Jesus has you.

Eden

I was a clever little one. One day in kindergarten, I decided it would be a good idea to run away before class started. I ran out the school doors and into the parking lot, where I found my dad. Thankfully, he brought me home. But when we got there, my mom was not happy. She took me right back to school!

My teacher explained to my mom that she had been worried because she saw me, then she didn't. She explained the responsibility she felt to keep me safe in her classroom because she loved me. I knew she meant it and felt bad for escaping.

It's the same for us as teens. Our teachers, parents, and coaches want to keep us. Because they love and care for us, they want to hold us close. They can feel like "helicopter adults" at times. They might not let us go to that party, make it mandatory to spend time with family, or dish out consequences that don't make sense at the time. Although they can be a pain sometimes, they love us. They enforce boundaries and consequences for our good.

Jesus is like this too. He loves us so much that He chases us again and again when we run away. Ultimately, He wants us for Himself. When we abandon Him, He comes running after us. Even when we ignore Him, He keeps pursuing us.

When we feel unsafe, He is our safe haven. The fact that He keeps us proves we are His.

Reflection & Discussion Time

- How is living like "I got this" different from living like "God's got this"?
- Being kept means you are always going to be God's child. How does that impact how you view challenges and struggles?

You also were included in Christ when you heard the message of truth, the gospel of your salvation. When you believed, you were marked in him with a seal, the promised Holy Spirit, who is a deposit guaranteeing our inheritance.

EPHESIANS 1:13-14, NIV

DAY 18

I Am Sealed

Eric

This week we've talked about how the moment you placed your faith in Jesus, you were justified. God saved you from your sin and for your Savior, who will never let you go. Today's verses tell you more about what happened to you when you believed in Jesus, and it is really awesome news. Read the verses again and answer these questions:

- Who is the seal you were marked with?

- What does the Holy Spirit guarantee?

The moment you believed, the Holy Spirit moved into your life. You were sealed with the Holy Spirit, marked forever as belonging to God because the Spirit of God moved into your life.

Let's talk about kings and water bottles to help us think about what it means to be sealed.

Kings: In ancient times, a letter could be sealed with the signet ring of a king—to show that the letter was under the authority of the king and its message could not be changed. You were sealed by the Holy Spirit, showing you are under the authority of the King of kings.

Water bottles: If you ever travel out of the country—on a mission trip, for example—you might hear someone say, "Only drink the water if the seal is on the bottle. If it is sealed, you are good." The seal ensures that the contents in the container are untainted, that the water is pure. You are sealed with the Spirit. You are kept pure and protected by Him.

As a teenager, you likely hear a lot about self-confidence . . . perhaps that you need more of it. Having no confidence is miserable, but pursuing self-confidence can be miserable too because you are forced to put so much pressure on yourself. The Christian view of confidence is not confidence in the self but confidence in the Spirit. Confidence in the Spirit is better than confidence in the self. You can be confident because the Spirit of God has sealed your life, and you are never alone!

Eden

I am currently taking Latin. By the time you're reading this, I will be in AP Latin (how scary). In the first year of Latin, we learned how merchants and Roman men would seal letters and agreements with a signet ring. Basically, it's a stamp that signifies ownership. It claims something to be true and authentically theirs.

I really like how the NLT version of the Bible translates

Ephesians 1:13: "And when you believed in Christ, he identified you as his own by giving you the Holy Spirit, whom he promised long ago." How amazing is it that He "identified me as his own"? He said, "She's mine!"

I really did not like being separated from my mom when I was little and would wait expectantly for her to come back to church or preschool to pick me up. The moment she showed up at the door, pointed to me, and said, "She's mine," was just the best. She could have pointed at any kid and said that, but it wouldn't have been true. But when she pointed at me, we both knew it was true. I knew because she gave me life, fed me, hugged me when I was sad, tucked me in at night, and woke me in the mornings. I was definitely hers!

How do we know we are God's? Because He gave us a gift. When He said, "She's mine" or "He's mine," we received the gift of the Holy Spirit. God *with* us! God not only identified us as His but gave us Himself! I know I am His in a lot of ways, but a big one is conviction. When I mess up (and I mess up a lot), the Holy Spirit inside of me points out my failure but, at the same time, shows me grace to bring me back. That's supernatural and could only come from Him. The Holy Spirit comforts me during heartbreak and pain in a way that no one else could. He gives me a peace that I can't put into words. I am definitely His!

Reflection & Discussion Time

- Think of a time the Holy Spirit convicted you that you'd done something wrong. What did you do with that conviction?
- How would remembering God is with you wherever you go impact your confidence?

Thanks be to God! He gives us the victory through our Lord Jesus Christ.

1 CORINTHIANS 15:57, NIV

You have already won a victory . . . because the Spirit who lives in you is greater than the spirit who lives in the world.

1 JOHN 4:4

DAY 19

I Am Victorious

Eric

Before I became a Christian, I was an absolute mess. I was arrested in high school for stealing credit cards from cars and going through the city where I grew up buying beer with a few friends. I had to stand in front of a judge when I was seventeen, knees knocking, nervous about the sentence I would receive. I heard "six months suspended sentence," which I knew meant probation. I was so relieved. But imagine my response if I had been declared not guilty, even though I *was* guilty. Even more than that, imagine if the judge had said, "Not guilty—*and* here is a new car." That's what we got when Jesus declared us justified, which we have been talking about this week. We were fully forgiven *and* we received much—His righteousness, His Spirit, and His victory—as Jesus is the One who conquered death when He rose from the dead.

And check this out! God declared you righteous and justified you at the *beginning* of your journey as a Christian. He does not wait until the end of your life. He has already given the verdict!

You already have the victory over sin and death and shame because Jesus' victory is yours.

You don't live *for* victory, but you get to live *from* victory.

Let me explain with a story. I coached my youngest daughter's soccer team when she was five, which was really not soccer but instead a massive blob of kids following the ball around. The kids' favorite game—the game they played the best, the game they played with the most confidence—was a game where the other team did not have enough players and had to forfeit. The referee called the game and declared us the winners, then asked if we still wanted to play. We'd already won the game, but we were invited to play anyway. Some of the other team's missing players finally showed up, but it did not matter. We had already been declared the winners. The kids loved that game. They played from victory and not for victory.

If you follow Jesus, you already have the victory. The One who keeps you has risen from the dead. The Spirit who has sealed you and lives within you is greater than the world. You can do your best in school, in athletics, and in your hopes and dreams without the pressure of having to prove yourself. You can do your best because you are already victorious where it matters most.

Eden

If I am honest, doing well in school has been a source of pride for me. My desire to do well has, at times, become an idol, or the most important thing in my life. The thought of making anything less than an A has destroyed me. My parents in their wisdom offered to pay me to make a B, which I took great offense to! However, Jesus loves me so much that He continues to break this idol.

My junior year was extremely difficult academically, but once again I found pride in how great I was doing—until I made a huge mistake. I missed a bio test because I was sick and then put off taking it for longer than I was supposed to, which caused me to receive a 20 percent deduction from my grade. So my test score, which would have been a 98 percent, fell to 78 percent, which is a huge deal in a class that has few tests. I suddenly felt the pain of not being able to be victorious on my own. I was so frustrated with myself and my teacher over this huge consequence. I set up a meeting with my teacher and our dean of students and presented my case on why I should get back my 20 percent. While they were super kind, they did not budge.

I was devastated but deep down knew this was probably one of the best lessons I could ever learn. My pride was broken. As the semester came to a close, I was shocked to receive an email from my teacher saying, "I have decided to give you back the 20 percent you lost at the beginning of the semester." The victory I couldn't win for myself was graciously given to me. I didn't deserve it. I messed up, and the consequence was fair.

As teens, there are times where we get good things we don't deserve. Think about when a teacher raises a grade that didn't deserve to be raised, or when we get playing time in a game when we weren't performing well at practice. We are overwhelmed by the kindness of our teachers and coaches in these moments because we know we don't deserve it.

It is the same with our relationship with God. His goodness, forgiveness, and victory over sin are gifts we don't deserve and did nothing to earn. We don't need to worry if sin has the final victory over our lives because Jesus already won. We may go through hard things, but we can rest in Jesus' victory over death.

Living from victory, not for victory, is so powerful for me to remember. I am an achiever. I like to win! But with Jesus it's different. I don't have to be perfect or earn my way. All I need to do is trust Him, and He will make a way. As teens, we face a lot of pressure from different people telling us how to live. I don't have to fear or be overwhelmed by the idea of succeeding or performing, because Jesus Christ already holds the victory in my life.

Reflection & Discussion Time

- What is the difference between "living for victory" and "living from victory"?
- What is one area of your life where you need God's help living from victory?

He gave his life to free us from every kind of sin,
to cleanse us, and to make us his very own people,
totally committed to doing good deeds.

TITUS 2:14

DAY 20

I Am Cleansed

Eric

When I was a college student, I was asked to speak at an event for teenagers. I invited my college roommate, Lance, to come with me. On the way there, I made the unwise decision to stop at a barbecue place. As I consumed a brisket sandwich, I spilled a ton of barbecue sauce on the shirt I was going to wear while speaking.

Lance is a solid friend, and he said, "Hey, man, let's trade shirts in the bathroom when we are done."

I was like, "No way, you aren't the one who made this mess. It's on me."

"Eric, I am not letting my best friend look like that when he speaks at this thing."

Lance showed up at the event looking like the idiot who can't eat a sandwich, and I showed up spotless.

Lance is a good friend to me, and Jesus is an even better friend to you. He took your stained life, and He wore it on the cross. He gave you His perfect clothes. He fully cleansed you.

According to today's verse, Jesus gave His life to accomplish three things in your life. (Fill in the blanks below.)

- To free us from ....
- To .... us
- To make us ....

Because of what Jesus has accomplished for us, we are to be "totally committed to doing good deeds." He has cleansed you, so you should live as if you have been cleansed. His cleansing of your sin should impact how you act with friends, how you talk at school, and how you react to others. He has freed you from every kind of sin, so don't run back to what you've been set free from! Jesus has made you His very own, so your life should look like you belong to Him.

Eden

One time when I was babysitting, the kids were playing in the dirt outside. It was funny for a while. However, once I cleaned them, they just ran outside and got dirty again. They even got dirt on me as I cleaned them off. I was frustrated that I'd cleaned them just so they could get dirty again. If you have spent time with little kids, you can probably relate.

Sometimes I spend time cleaning our house only to come back to a mess. Who knows who the culprit was. It could have been my dad, my dog, or even my sister! It's really not fun to clean a mess just to come right back to another one.

See, this is what Jesus did for us! He washed us clean and wore our sin when He died on the cross. When we trust Jesus to be our Savior, we are cleaned from the inside. We are not merely a better person but a brand-new one. We are washed of all our sin. We shouldn't go back to our old ways because Jesus calls us to live a new way.

Becoming a Christian does not mean a full transformation overnight. It means your desires will change over time. Everything changes when we stop desiring things of this world and start desiring Jesus. For a teen, it may seem so hard to let go of the world. It's the big and small things that we just want to hang on to. I'm speaking from experience! I trust God so much, so why do I continue to worry about His plan for my life? I truly believe I am who Jesus says I am, so why do I still sometimes seek the approval of others? These moments are a reminder that He is still working on me. The truth is none of us are perfect. But the closer you grow to Jesus and the more time you spend in His Word, the less you'll desire things of this world.

Reflection & Discussion Time

- How has being cleansed by God changed you?
- As one of God's people, what are some good deeds you could do to show His love to others?

It is for freedom that Christ has set us free.
Stand firm, then, and do not let yourselves be
burdened again by a yoke of slavery.

GALATIANS 5:1, NIV

DAY 21

I Am Free

Eric

Today's verse was written to a group of people who were being told they had to obey certain religious rules to get God to love them. As Christians, we obey because God has already set us free, not because we think He will set us free if we do what He says. When you became a Christian, Christ set you free from many things that can enslave you, rob you of joy and peace, and cause you to be miserable.

Below is a list of some common traps that can enslave us. Circle the ones that you experience most often:

- living for others to approve of you
- trying to find happiness apart from God
- desiring to be seen as powerful or popular
- focusing on accomplishments and never slowing down to listen to God
- feeling like you need to be in control

- worrying about your future or if you will be successful
- comparing yourself to others

How do these traps impact you? Write about it below.

Because Christ took all your sin upon Himself, to go back to what enslaved you is to go back to something you know does not satisfy you. You are free! You don't need to go back. Remind yourself that Christ is better, that He has made you free, and "if the Son sets you free, you will be free indeed" (John 8:36, NIV).

Eden

Over the past year, I have learned a lot about myself. I'm so thankful Jesus has shown me who I am in Him, but I've learned other things about myself too—things about my personality. I love taking personality tests. They are so fun! Most personality tests don't just show your strengths, though—they show your weaknesses too. Sadly, every time I read the results, I know that the poor character qualities are brutally true.

When I look at the list above, I can easily identify what enslaves me. I know that I often live for others' approval, and I spend lots of time trying to accomplish perfection. I care so much for people (which is a good thing), but I can care too much about what they think about me (bad thing). This usually ends up coming back to bite me. I also struggle with feeling like I need to be the best at everything, which never happens. These traps always leave me empty. No matter what you struggle with, there are traps that can enslave each of us and hold us back from taking chances and getting out of our comfort zone. These traps can even keep us from knowing who God is and what He is calling us to do for Him. Do you know why? Because we are too focused on ourselves to hear from Him. I know this from experience. But Jesus tells us we don't need to be enslaved to these things. We have been set free and can live in that freedom.

Reflection & Discussion Time

- What tends to pull you away from living free in Christ?
- How can you remind yourself daily that Christ has set you free?

Memory Verse

Praise be to the God and Father of our Lord Jesus Christ, who has blessed us in the heavenly realms with every spiritual blessing in Christ.

EPHESIANS 1:3, NIV

WEEK FOUR

I Am with God and for God

They stumble because they do not obey God's word, and so they meet the fate that was planned for them. But you are not like that, for you are a chosen people. You are royal priests.

1 PETER 2:8-9

DAY 22

I Am His Priest (Part 1)

Eric

"A priest!? I'm not a priest!" When most people hear the word *priest*, they think of someone who wears one of those religious collars, promises to never get married, and works at a church. But when the Bible says followers of Jesus are priests, it is emphasizing an awesome truth about who you are. As today's verses say, you are not like those who don't know God. You are chosen by God for a special job. In the Old Testament, before Jesus entered our world, being a priest was an amazing privilege and a profound responsibility. Today we will talk about the privilege, and tomorrow the responsibility.

People often envy celebrities because of where they can go and who they can see. They go backstage at major concerts to hang out with the artists or into the locker room of big games to meet the players. Being a priest is also about where you can go and who you can be with. But it is way better than being a celebrity.

In Old Testament times, the Temple was the center of life for God's people. The largest part of the Temple complex was the outer court, and you had to be born a Jew to go there. The second-largest area was the Holy Place, and to go there you had to be a priest who was a descendant of Aaron. The most sacred part of the Temple was the Most Holy Place, where God's presence would meet with man at the mercy seat, which was the lid of the Ark of the Covenant. Only one person, the high priest, could go into this sacred area, and only one day a year—the Day of Atonement. People wondered what it would be like to be that priest, to spend time with the God of the universe, to be able to talk with God. People dreamed of being that person.

You are that person. You can enter into the presence of God.

When Jesus died, the curtain that blocked off the Most Holy Place was ripped in two (see Matthew 27:51). God does not meet with people in the Temple anymore. He will meet with you anytime and anywhere because you are His priest. Here's what the book of Hebrews tells us:

> And so, dear brothers and sisters, we can boldly enter heaven's Most Holy Place because of the blood of Jesus. By his death, Jesus opened a new and life-giving way through the curtain into the Most Holy Place.
>
> HEBREWS 10:19-20

You get to be with God, talk to Him, and hear from Him! You are His priest!

Eden

We all know there are privileges that come with certain roles. Even as teens, we experience this. There are privileges I get because my dad is a pastor. Sometimes I get to swim in the baptismal pool and eat the snacks that are supposed to be for the preacher (shhh, don't rat me out!). When my mom was a teacher, I would get to ride my Segway down the hallways and eat candy from my mom's stash. Although my parents are normal people, there are cool parts that come with their jobs.

Like my dad wrote above, priests in the Old Testament had many privileges, but only one priest could be in God's presence in the Holy of Holies—and only once a year! Now that Jesus has given us access, we can be in God's presence anytime!

As a teen, sometimes I wonder how I can hear God's voice. I always feel like others can hear Him so much better than I can. In those discouraging moments, I remember that God has already spoken. I can read Scripture and know I am reading His words—words that are still meant for me today. I don't need a title or a special job to speak to the Lord or hear from Him. Because of Jesus, I get to talk to Him anywhere and anytime.

Reflection & Discussion Time

- If a friend asked you what the Bible means when it calls us priests, what would you say?
- When and where could be a time and place for you to meet with God in prayer?

You are living stones that God is building into his spiritual temple. What's more, you are his holy priests. Through the mediation of Jesus Christ, you offer spiritual sacrifices that please God.

1 PETER 2:5

DAY 23

I Am His Priest (Part 2)

Eric

Yesterday we talked about the privilege of being His priest—that you can meet with God anytime and anywhere. Today, let's talk about the responsibility of being His priest. In Old Testament times, the priest represented the people to God by offering sacrifices for them and praying to God for them. The priest also represented God to the people by giving them an example of someone who follows God. You have the same responsibility!

You bring people before God.

In Old Testament times, the high priest would go before God and plead for His mercy for the people and bring the requests of the people before God. If he was a good priest, he passionately prayed to God for the people because he loved them. As you spend time with God in prayer, you can do the same thing. Pray for your friends, your family, and your classmates and teammates. Pray for their struggles and challenges. Ask God to work in their lives.

You bring God before people.

One of the expectations of a priest was to show God's character to people, to give people an example of what it looks like to follow God. As a Christian, you have the responsibility to show Jesus to the world. People were first called Christians because of their reputation as followers of Jesus—they were like mini versions of Christ. The good news is that when you spend time with God in prayer, He will make you more like Him. You don't have to give yourself a speech about how you should "do better." If you stay close to God, He will keep changing you with His love, joy, and holiness. You will show up at school, work, and practice differently because you have been with God.

You are His priest. Enjoy being in His presence!

Eden

I am a pretty amazing matchmaker, a great wing-woman (that means I'm good at making my friend's crush like her back)! You know how this works: you talk very highly about your friend in front of her crush and then tell her what he said. You foster the relationship between the two.

Priests were kind of like this, but never in a shady or awkward way! They would foster the relationship between God and the people. They would pray for the people and on their behalf. We are called to do this today as teens. It's often easy to pray for ourselves and our own struggles, but it's hard to pray for someone who has hurt us. It may even be hard to pray for our friends. Everyone likes talking about themselves, but we are called to pray for others for a few reasons. First, it's humbling and moves our focus from ourselves and onto God. Second, there is power in prayer. We should pray on behalf of our brothers and sisters in Christ, knowing our prayers make an impact. Jesus is so kind to let us pray and then watch as He works. This builds our faith too.

We are also like priests in the way we represent God to others. People look to us to understand the Christian life. We are called to be set apart from the rest of the world. How can we expect to bring people to Jesus if we act like everyone else? People often have trouble with Christianity because the people they look to as representatives talk and act the same as everyone else. As teens who belong to God, we need to act differently by radiating the love of Christ.

Reflection & Discussion Time

- Spend some time thanking God for who He is. Write down some things about Him that you are thankful for.
- Spend some time praying for the people in your life. Write down the names of these people and what you are praying for.

In Christ you have been brought to fullness.

COLOSSIANS 2:10, NIV

Praise be to the God and Father of our Lord Jesus Christ, who has blessed us in the heavenly realms with every spiritual blessing in Christ.

EPHESIANS 1:3, NIV

DAY 24

I Am in Christ

Eric

Underline the phrase "in Christ" in today's verses.

The phrase "in Christ" is common in the Bible to describe our close relationship with Jesus. When God the Spirit moves into our life, we are "in Christ." Jesus told His disciples that after He died, rose from the dead, and ascended into heaven, they would receive the Spirit and they "would be in Him and He in them":

> I will ask the Father, and he will give you another advocate to help you and be with you forever—the Spirit of truth. . . . On that day you will realize that I am in my Father, and you are in me, and I am in you.
>
> JOHN 14:16-17, 20, NIV

You are in Christ and He is in you, and that changes everything.

You are in school, but you are also in Christ. You are at your job, but you are also in Christ. You are in a group of friends, but you are also in Christ. You are in your culture, but you are also in Christ. You are not always in those other places, but you are always in Christ.

A way to help you visualize this is to get two oranges and a large jar or bucket of water. Peel one of the oranges until there is no peel left. Drop them both in the water. The orange that is still in the peel will float. The orange that is outside the peel will sink. Both oranges are in the water, but the orange that is also in the peel is not submerged or overwhelmed.

You are always in Him, and though you are also in the world, the world will not overcome you!

Eden

The idea of one day being pregnant and carrying a baby scares me. You are carrying a living being in your body! If your parents are anything like mine, they have told you what you were like as a baby. They may have even told stories from when you were in your mom's womb. My mom told me that I went to Hawaii with my parents when I was in her womb. She has said, "Baby Eden was inside Mrs. Kaye in Hawaii!" Weird!

What is amazing, though, is that everywhere I went in my mom's womb, I was covered and protected by my mom's body. Christians are in Christ. We are covered by Him, surrounded by Him. We are called to live in the world but not be conformed to the world. We can only accomplish this because we are *in Him*. As we go to school and sports and other activities, we don't have to conform to the way of life of those around us. Instead, we can live in the world while still remembering that we are always in Christ. Christ is in us, and we are in Him! So, as we go through our daily routines, we can live differently. Because like that orange in the peel, the world doesn't consume us because we are covered in the Holy Spirit.

Reflection & Discussion Time

- Why is it easier to remember that you are in the world than it is to remember that you are in Christ?
- In your daily life, what would it look like to live differently from the world around you?

James, a servant of God and of the Lord Jesus Christ . . .

JAMES 1:1, NIV

Jude, a servant of Jesus Christ . . .

JUDE 1:1, NIV

Paul, a servant of Christ Jesus . . .

ROMANS 1:1, NIV

DAY 25

I Am His Servant

Eric

What do you want to be known for? When you meet someone for the first time, what do you lead with? Maybe it is the sport you play, the school you attend, or something you have accomplished. Those topics are very common. What is uncommon is how the early Christians introduced themselves in the letters they wrote.

James, Jude, and Paul could have introduced themselves as authors of books, the world's greatest missionaries, spiritual entrepreneurs, people well-known throughout history, or respected leaders. All those are true, but they went with "servant." Even more amazing is that Jude and James were brothers of Jesus. They did not name-drop Jesus as their brother as in "beat Jesus in a race as a kid," but instead they called themselves His servants, showing that they lived to honor Jesus. My younger brother would *never* say that about me!

They chose the low title of servant because they had learned that the low title is the best title.

James and Jude found their ultimate identity not in that they shared a house or meal with Jesus, but that they followed Him and worshiped Him. They belonged to Jesus' earthly family, but their more important identity was that they were in His spiritual family. The earthly family is temporary, but the spiritual family is forever. We enter His spiritual family by becoming His servant, and we enjoy the Christian life by living as His servant.

Other titles in your life will come and go. You won't always be a student or a volleyball player. But you will always be a servant of Christ, and that is the best title. You get to serve Him through all the roles He has given you. As you do your homework, you are ultimately doing it for Him. As you participate in activities, do your best because you are really serving Him.

Eden

I love serving now, but I didn't always feel that way! I hate to say I didn't get the point when I was younger. My parents encouraged me to find a way to serve, and when I found my church's disability ministry, I knew that was my place. Serving every weekend with the best kids ever is so life-giving. Serving has made the idea of being the "hands and feet of Jesus" come to life for me. Serving helps me practice humility, reminding me that life is not all about me.

Serving is good for teenagers, and lots of people know it! Some schools even require students to put in a certain number of service hours per year. The danger in this is that if we serve just to complete a service hours requirement, we might lose the heart behind serving. However, do I think Jesus can use any service opportunity to change our hearts? Absolutely!

We are not servants of the Lord only when we are completing our service hours or volunteering in a church ministry. As Christians, we are always servants. At school, we can work hard to serve the Lord with our studies. In sports, we can show good sportsmanship and treat our coaches with respect. Everything we do is to glorify Him and make Him known. When we serve, we often find joy and gratitude because we take the focus off ourselves.

Reflection & Discussion Time

- What would you say if someone asked you: "Why is it a good thing to be God's servant?"
- Where are some places you can serve God?

Just as our bodies have many parts and each part has a special function, so it is with Christ's body. We are many parts of one body, and we all belong to each other.

In his grace, God has given us different gifts for doing certain things well. So if God has given you the ability to prophesy, speak out with as much faith as God has given you. If your gift is serving others, serve them well. If you are a teacher, teach well. If your gift is to encourage others, be encouraging. If it is giving, give generously. If God has given you leadership ability, take the responsibility seriously. And if you have a gift for showing kindness to others, do it gladly.

ROMANS 12:4-8

DAY 26

I Am Gifted

Eric

Have you ever noticed how one small injury on your body impacts everything? A few years ago, I got tennis elbow from working out, and it was horrible. One small tendon in my body wasn't functioning as it should, and it felt like my whole body was messed up. God says you are an important part of His body—so important that the body is not the same without you.

When you became a Christian and His Spirit moved into your life, He gifted you with at least one spiritual gift. You have a supernatural ability, given to you by God to serve other people in His body, the church. You are a valuable member of God's body. Your gift is not meant to make you look good; it's meant to benefit others. In the Scripture passage at the top of the page, underline all the spiritual gifts that are mentioned.

People love to try to figure out what their spiritual gifts are. The lists of spiritual gifts in the Bible are not exhaustive. They're meant to be examples of the kinds of gifts God gives. When I was in college, I went to a conference where they passed out a spiritual gifts test. Two of the gifts listed were martyrdom and celibacy. As I was taking the test, I tried to reverse-engineer my answers so I didn't end up with those two gifts. Martyrdom is a gift you can just use one time. I want to use my gift more than once. And celibacy . . . well, it is a passive gift, and I thought I was more prone to active gifts. *God, I am on your team, but if you can give me a position on the court other than a celibate martyr, I would love that.*

I have learned that the best way for you to discover where you're most gifted is to try the gifts out! Tests can be helpful, but they are not found in the Bible. What is found in the Bible are commands to serve. Dive into serving, and as you serve, God will reveal to you how He has gifted you. Volunteer in a role at your church! You will inspire others as you serve, but God will also teach you about how He has gifted you.

Eden

As I mentioned before, I love taking personality tests. Spiritual gift tests can also be helpful and fun to take and talk about with your friends. However, serving is definitely what has helped me determine where Jesus has gifted me. The more I serve, the more obvious my gifts have become, which in turn gives me the desire to serve more!

Jesus has shown me my main spiritual gifts are encouraging others, discernment, and hospitality. It's been cool to see how God has used these gifts in my life. I love encouraging other people to grow, and I have seen that gift used as I serve kids with disabilities. It's so rewarding to pour into these special kids and their families. The gift of discernment has helped me make wise decisions in life about school and relationships. When I listen to the Spirit through prayer and reading Scripture, He gives me wisdom. I also love being hospitable to others, and I am using that spiritual gift as I host a Bible study for teenagers at my house.

No one spiritual gift is better than any other. They are all important, and God uses every gift. I encourage you to start serving, even as a teen. God wants to use you now, and by serving you will learn what gifts He has given you. But don't treat your gifts as excuses to get out of obeying God in areas that are harder for you. Just because generosity is challenging for me does not mean I should not be generous. Just because evangelism doesn't come easily to me does not mean I should not share God's Word with others. And a person who's not as gifted at hospitality can't use that as an excuse to slam the door in someone's face! We can't use a spiritual-gifts list to stop us from loving people, serving people, and sharing God's Word with others.

Reflection & Discussion Time

- Take a look at the spiritual gifts listed in Romans 12:4-8. Which of these can you identify in your own life? Which ones are harder for you?
- Are there some ministries in your church where you could volunteer to serve others? What could you do to learn more about them or express interest in serving?

Just as each one has received a gift, use it to serve others, as good stewards of the varied grace of God. If anyone speaks, let it be as one who speaks God's words; if anyone serves, let it be from the strength God provides, so that God may be glorified through Jesus Christ in everything. To him be the glory and the power forever and ever. Amen.

1 PETER 4:10-11, CSB

DAY 27

I Am a Steward of His Grace

Eric

When you hear the word *stewardship*, what do you think of? Write down some things that come to your mind:

Stewardship is carefully caring for the resources God has given you. Another word for *stewardship* is *management*, and many people think of finances, time, opportunities, and resources when they hear those two words. All of those things are important, and thinking of yourself as a steward of those is good because it shows you believe God is the owner. He owns it all, and He gives us those gifts to manage—to steward.

But today's verse blows my mind. I never thought of this part of stewardship until I studied this verse. It says you steward God's grace! God wants His grace managed and given to others, and He has decided that His people will steward it for Him. You steward His grace by using your gifts. God has grace He wants to give to people, and He is going to do that through the gifts He's given you.

And today's verse says "each one" has received a gift. That means you too! Some scholars point out that the Bible lists two types of gifts: *speaking gifts* and *serving gifts*.

SPEAKING GIFTS	SERVING GIFTS
Teaching	Hospitality
Exhorting	Mercy
Prophecy	Helping
Wisdom	Giving
Leading	Administrating

All of these gifts are very important and help people know and experience God's grace in different ways. As we talked about yesterday, the best way to learn where you're gifted is to just start serving. Using your gift is thrilling. You will love it! But God gave you the gift you have received to serve others, to give His grace to others. You have been gifted by Him, for them.

Eden

When I was in elementary school, we had a "gifted program" for kids who were extra-smart. I still rack my brain trying to understand why they called it "gifted" and not "advanced" or "honors." I was not in the gifted program. When I found out that I wasn't considered gifted and that some of my friends were, it was a little discouraging, even for a second grader. But no matter if your school calls you gifted or not, Jesus does! Jesus tells us that He has given each of us gifts to use for Him.

Jesus gives us the power to use our gifts to glorify Him and show His grace to those around us. I kind of can't get over this. *Grace* means undeserved approval or favor. We get to give that out to others as we use our gifts. No matter what gift you have been given and whether or not you feel like it's one of the more important gifts, God uses all gifts for His glory. They are all used to show His grace. So cool! This means when I use my gift of hospitality to have people over and make them feel welcome and loved at my house, I am showing God's grace to them. When you serve using your gifts, it's so fun! It can be hard to put yourself out there and use the gifts God has given you. It was not easy for me! But when you do, you will not regret it.

As a teen, how can you practically use your gifts? Well, it's easier than you think. Get involved in your church, in your community, or even in a Bible club at school (or start one)! Jesus will make His desire your heart's desire if you are following Him. The closer we grow to Jesus, the more what we want will begin to match what He wants for us. What I do know is that He wants you to use your gifts because it's good for you and for those around you. I challenge you to be bold and ask God where He wants to use you and see what happens!

Reflection & Discussion Time

- How does it make you feel that God shows His grace to others through you?
- Which spiritual gifts do you see in the lives of your friends or family members? Let them know how these gifts have helped or encouraged you!

Clearly, you are a letter from Christ showing the result of our ministry among you. This "letter" is written not with pen and ink, but with the Spirit of the living God. It is carved not on tablets of stone, but on human hearts.

2 CORINTHIANS 3:3

DAY 28

I Am Christ's Living Letter

Eric

You are more than halfway through this devotional, which is huge. Spending time reading God's Word, even if you have missed days and then picked back up where you left off, is evidence that God is working in your life. He is pursuing you. He is changing you. You are His priest, so you are spending time with Him and you are representing Him to others. You are His servant, so He has gifted you to serve, and He is planning to partner with you to impact other people. I am excited for you! Well done! Keep going.

While you are reading the Bible, many others are not—at least not yet. Dwight Moody is commonly credited with saying, "Out of 100 men, one will read the Bible; the other 99 will read the Christian." People are reading your life. This is why Scripture says you are "a letter from Christ." Not a letter written with a pen in a notebook or with a stylus on an iPad, but with God's Spirit on your heart. When a Christian serves someone in Christ's name, their serving is a living example of how Christ serves us. When a Christian forgives someone who has wronged him or her, their forgiveness is a letter showing how God forgives us.

When people read the Bible, they learn about God's love, kindness, power, holiness, and so much more. What are people learning about God by reading your life?

Eden

Reading has never been my favorite. So when a movie is produced based on a popular book, I much prefer to watch the movie. I'm sure I'm not the only one. A lot of teenagers would prefer the movie to the book. Likewise, more teenagers are going to watch the lives of Christians rather than read the Bible that the Christians believe.

Of course we should read the Bible and encourage others to do the same! But in order to reach those who won't pick up a Bible, we also need to represent Christ well. People need to be able to learn about God's joy by seeing our joy, God's kindness to people by our kindness to people, and God's commitment to truth by our own truthfulness. May people who look at us wonder why we are different, joyful, and filled with peace, and then may they ask us why!

I don't think we realize the impact we can have on others. Our actions can reflect Christ and bring others to Him. Think about your Instagram page, what you wear, the way you talk, and what you do on weekends. If someone followed you around for a day, what would they gather? As a Christian, we represent Christ. It's a big deal! I pray that Jesus will keep my heart focused on Him so that I make wise decisions that point others to Him.

Reflection & Discussion Time

- In what areas of your life do you feel you represent Christ well?
- Where do you need His forgiveness and His help so you can better represent Him to others?

Memory Verse

If anyone is in Christ, the new creation has come: The old has gone, the new is here!

2 CORINTHIANS 5:17, NIV

WEEK FIVE

I Should Not Always Fit In

Dear friends, I urge you as strangers and exiles to abstain from sinful desires that wage war against the soul. Conduct yourselves honorably among [those who do not know God], so that when they slander you as evildoers, they will observe your good works and will glorify God on the day he visits.

1 PETER 2:11-12, CSB

DAY 29

I Am a Stranger

Eric

Do you ever feel like you don't fully fit in? Like you are a bit on the outside of some jokes, how some people think, or some of the things people at your school talk about doing?

If so, good! If you don't feel like you always fit in because of your faith, then you are growing in your relationship with God and showing those around you that there is more than this world. I know not fitting in may not always feel good, but it is good! You are not supposed to feel like you fully belong in this world because you don't. If you've become a follower of Jesus, this world is no longer your home. The apostle Peter wrote the above passage to Christians throughout the Roman Empire. The emperor, Nero, had even falsely accused Christians of starting a fire that greatly damaged Rome. Peter reminded them that they were "strangers and exiles," that this world would not make them happy and that they did not fully belong here. Notice how Peter challenged them in the passage, and then consider the following questions:

- What do these verses say we are to do with our sinful desires?

- What do these verses say we are to do among those who do not know God?

Some Christians stay away from people who don't know God yet give in to their own sinful desires. The Scripture says to do the opposite. Stay away from sinful desires and set a good example among those who do not yet believe. Another way to say it is: duel your sin inwardly and display your Savior outwardly.

You are different, so live differently by fighting your own selfish and sinful desires. You are different, so live differently in front of people who are watching to see what makes you different.

Eden

Have you ever stayed in a motel? Well, I have, and I would prefer *not* to stay in a motel. But I find comfort in knowing that it is only temporary. I get to go home to my house! I love traveling, but I am such a homebody and love my own bed even more. See, a motel is like the world. It is our temporary home—our forever home is with Jesus. We aren't always going to live in this world, and everything it has to offer is only temporary.

While we are here, what matters the most is people. They are the one thing we can "take with us" to heaven. Some "religious" people think we shouldn't be friends with people who party, sleep around, or make unwise decisions. But that is not true. Think about the people Jesus was friends with. Jesus sat and ate with sinners and tax collectors, yet He was perfect and without sin. Of course, He was Jesus! I want to show Jesus to those who don't know Him, while at the same time being wise. I realize to fight my own sinful desires I must surround myself with those who build me up and keep me accountable as well. Yes, it is important to be friends with those who do not yet know Jesus. And yes, it is also important that my biggest influences are those who encourage me to grow in my faith.

Reflection & Discussion Time

- When have you have felt out of place as a Christian? Why did you feel that way?
- Why is it important for us to duel sin? What sins are you currently fighting in your life?

I have given them your word. The world hated them because they are not of the world, just as I am not of the world. I am not praying that you take them out of the world but that you protect them from the evil one. They are not of the world, just as I am not of the world.

JOHN 17:14-16, CSB

DAY 30

I Am Not of This World

Eric

What is Jesus doing right now? Have you thought about that? According to the Bible, He is praying for you right now—as "he lives forever to intercede with God" for His people (Hebrews 7:25). Jesus is praying for you as you go to school, as you hang out with your friends, through your highs and lows, and in the midst of all your trials.

That has to make you wonder what He's praying! What is Jesus, God the Son, asking God the Father for on your behalf? There might be a clue in the prayer Jesus prayed in the garden of Gethsemane before He went to the cross. He prayed for His disciples, and He prays for us. Part of that prayer is the above Scripture, our passage for today.

Jesus says His own are not of this world. He actually prays that phrase twice in today's verses. Answer these questions about what else you see in this passage:

- What has Jesus given His disciples?

- How does the world feel about His disciples?

- What does Jesus pray for?

All of Jesus' disciples who were with Jesus in the garden were hated by the world. They experienced both incredible joy *and* immense suffering—joy because of Jesus and suffering because the world persecuted them. Church history tells us that ten of them were killed and one, John, was exiled to an island. Though they paid a great price for their faith, every one of them believed Jesus was better than whatever they sacrificed. They kept preaching that Jesus was alive despite threats against them because they knew Jesus is greater than this world.

It can sound like Jesus' prayer that they would be protected from the evil one (Satan) was not answered, but it was. Because through all the trials the disciples faced, God held on to them and kept their faith strong. They were not of this world anyway! They finished this life holding on to the One who never stopped holding on to them. They are in everlasting paradise now, and the evil one will one day be banished. The evil one did not win and will not win.

You are not of the world either. When you feel out of place, just know that Jesus is praying for you and holding on to you.

Eden

I am left-handed—very left-handed. Unlike my sister, who's also technically left-handed, I do absolutely nothing right-handed. I kick with my left foot, serve with my left hand, shoot left-handed, and even have a left-handed guitar. Imagine the surprise and excitement I felt when my third-grade teacher, after viewing my terrible cutting, said, "Eden, why aren't you using left-handed scissors?"

There are left-handed scissors?! I had always cut with right-handed scissors in my left hand.

After school, I ran to my mom's classroom to tell her the great news because I felt sure she didn't know either. When I told my mom about the left-handed scissors, she looked at me with a smile and said, "I know about those, but you don't need them. It's better for you to learn to live as a lefty in a right-handed world. It will make you stronger." I was pretty annoyed at this. Cutting was so hard for me, and left-handed scissors would have changed all of that. What my mom meant, though, was that being different and set apart while living in a world that is uncomfortable would build my character. She was right. Most things aren't made for hardcore lefties like me, but I have persevered and learned. (My cutting could still be better!)

Being a Christian in a world that is not our home can often feel a lot like being a lefty in a right-handed world. If you try to do things the "right-handed way," they feel weird and wrong. This is because we are different, set apart just as Jesus was. It isn't always comfortable to be different—as a matter of fact, it's downright uncomfortable a lot of the time. Jesus gets it. It was the same for him.

Being different because of our faith is the best kind of different to be. What a great comfort to know Jesus is praying on our behalf! He is never the one who runs away, but the one who holds on to us. He never moves. When we feel like He is distant, it's because we have moved. He loves us so much that He pursues and brings us back. He is walking with us through life and praying for us along the way, so we never need to fear.

We know from Jesus that being a Christian is not easy. The fact that we don't belong to this world shows how hard it is. It's hard not to fall into the lifestyle of the world because we live in it. Being a Christian comes with sacrifice and lots of difficult decisions. When we are in them, it's often hard to see how our trials or difficulties could ever be used for good. But when we look back, sometimes we see where God was at work. Often, though, we can only see a little part of the picture in this life. If we could see everything God is doing, we would understand fully. One day we will!

Reflection & Discussion Time

- What does it mean to you that Jesus is praying for you right now?
- When have you felt like a left-handed person in a right-handed world? What did you learn from that experience?

You are God's slaves.

I PETER 2:16

Thank God! Once you were slaves of sin, but now you wholeheartedly obey this teaching we have given you. Now you are free from your slavery to sin, and you have become slaves to righteous living.

ROMANS 6:17-18

DAY 31

I Am a Slave to Righteousness

Eric

In America, we love being our own people. You hear statements like "You do you," "My truth," and "I'm going to find myself." The thinking is that we are fully in control of ourselves and have the power to make ourselves happy and fulfilled.

The Scripture says something shocking, something most people don't like at all. Here it is: None of us are completely independent. All of us are owned—either by sin or by righteousness.

That is the point of the above passage, which was written to Christians living in Rome during the early years of the Roman Empire. At that time, as many as a third of the people in Rome were slaves. It was not like the horrific slavery in US history where Black people were bought and sold because of their race, but those in slavery in Rome were still owned by someone else. Because slavery was something people saw every day, the apostle Paul used it to make a point that people would not miss.

Before you became a Christian, your sin owned you, bossed

you around, made promises to you and broke them, and hurt you. Now you are free from sin and are a slave to righteousness. You now live for God because He has taken away your sin and made you His own. You are not perfect. You don't always obey as you should, but He still owns you.

Below, write down what being a slave to sin brings someone versus what being a slave to God and righteousness brings someone.

Slave to Sin Brings:	**Slave to Righteousness Brings:**

Jesus is not a cruel Master. He is gracious, good, kind, and loving. He provides for you, cares for you, and has the power to work good things out of bad things in your life. But, of course, you don't fully fit into the world around you. You are not a slave to sin anymore!

Eden

I know I don't want to be a slave to anything. However, I sometimes feel like a slave to fear, control, people's opinions, or my own sin. But because of Jesus, I know none of those things can own me. I am learning the only way not to be a slave to those things is to be a slave to Jesus instead. Being a slave to Jesus is actually the only way to be free!

Sometimes the thought of being a slave to God scares me! One of the hardest things for me for a while was being able to say, "Lord, Your will be done! Use me how You want!" I was scared God was going to call me into something I didn't want to do. I was scared He would make me do something that is hard or scary. Now, I am not saying that won't happen. Jesus does ask teenagers to do difficult things for Him, and sometimes that's uncomfortable. But on the other side there is fruit that only comes through trials, and it is worth it!

Romans 6:17 talks about obeying God's teachings. In order to know how to do this, we have to be reading our Bibles. I have heard it said that to "displace a thought or fear that is not from Jesus, you must replace it with the truth of His Word." I know in my own life this is true!

Reflection & Discussion Time

- What are the damages you have seen of being a "slave to sin" in your own life or someone else's life?
- What are the benefits you have seen of being a "slave to righteousness"?

We are citizens of heaven, where the Lord Jesus Christ lives. And we are eagerly waiting for him to return as our Savior.

PHILIPPIANS 3:20

DAY 32

I Am a Citizen of Heaven

Eric

If you visit another country, you will likely notice customs and behaviors that are different from what you're used to. In the United Kingdom, it took me some time to get used to people driving on the left side of the road. In India, I could not order beef anywhere, even at a McDonald's! In Argentina, they served me yerba maté instead of coffee. In El Salvador, people took naps in the middle of the day (I did like that one). While different customs could seem strange to you as a visitor, they are normal to the people who are citizens of that country.

You are ultimately a citizen of Jesus' Kingdom, and the values in His Kingdom are different from the values of the world. As you are formed by His values, you will stand out more and more. And He will use you to bring the benefits of His Kingdom, His rule, to more people here and now.

The Kingdom we belong to—Jesus' Kingdom—has been called an upside-down Kingdom, meaning our values stand out in this world. Below are some of the "upside-down" values of Jesus' Kingdom. Circle the ones that you need to remind yourself of more often:

- To be first is to be last (Matthew 19:30).
- To be great is to be a servant (Matthew 20:26).
- To be strong is to be weak (2 Corinthians 12:9).
- To be poor in spirit is how to inherit the Kingdom of Heaven (Matthew 5:3).
- Love your enemies (Matthew 5:44).
- Humble yourself to be exalted (Luke 14:11).
- Store treasures in heaven, not on earth (Matthew 6:19-20).

Just as driving on the left side of the road required me to remind myself, *Stay left*, living these Kingdom values doesn't come naturally. We often have to remind ourselves that our values as Kingdom citizens are different from the values of this world. The longer I drove on the left side of the road, the more normal it became. And the longer you follow after Jesus, the more second nature and normal His values will be for you.

Eden

I was born in Florida and moved to Tennessee when I was almost four years old, and then to California when I was almost ten years old. Although I didn't move to a different country, I did notice many differences in the way people lived, sounded, and acted in California. I noticed the way people treated strangers in California was way different from how we did it in Nashville. Not better or worse, just different. People sounded different too, and I know for a fact they thought we sounded different! But one of the biggest differences was that most people didn't say, "Yes, ma'am" or "No, sir." When I first said those words to an adult in California, they thought I was being disrespectful. I felt terrible. I had to make sure my tone was super polite next time I addressed an adult that way because my parents weren't letting me quit.

If you have ever visited or moved to a new place, then you probably know what I'm talking about. These cultural differences have a lot to teach us about the Christian life. I hope people notice something different about us because of our citizenship in heaven! As Christians, we have certain characteristics and values. We go about life differently because we have been set apart by our Savior.

The main thing I need to remind myself of from the list above is "To be first is to be last." If you know me, then you know I like to be the best and first at everything. But truthfully, I don't need to be good at everything, and I don't need to be first. Instead, I need to humble myself and realize I cannot be good at everything. When life seems like it is going well, I have noticed it feels harder to rely on Jesus. I have to constantly remind myself that I am only good at things because they are gifts from Him. And even if I am not good at something, that is okay too, especially if it helps me depend more on God. This is just one of the cultural differences that sets us apart from the world.

Reflection & Discussion Time

- In today's devotional, why did you circle the Kingdom values you did? Why are those values challenging to live by?
- What values in Jesus' Kingdom are the most different, in your opinion, from those of this world?

[God[has enabled you to share in the inheritance that belongs to his people, who live in the light. For he has rescued us from the kingdom of darkness and transferred us into the Kingdom of his dear Son, who purchased our freedom and forgave our sins.

COLOSSIANS 1:12-14

DAY 33

I Am Transferred to the Kingdom of Light

Eric

Has a new kid ever transferred into your school? Maybe you have been the new kid! It seems everyone wants to know where the new kid came from and how he likes his new life compared to his old life. My wife and I moved my daughters from Nashville to Southern California when they were in elementary school, and they were the new kids for a while. Some people thought we upgraded moving to Southern California. Others thought we left the better place behind.

When you became a Christian, you were transferred from the kingdom of darkness to the Kingdom of Light. For sure an upgrade in every way. Satan is the leader of the kingdom of darkness, and there is only disappointment, shame, and despair in that kingdom. Jesus is the Leader of the Kingdom of Light, and the fruit of His Kingdom is love, joy, peace, patience, kindness, goodness, and self-control (see Galatians 5:22-23).

Notice today's verses, though. Did you transfer yourself or did

He transfer you? Using the wording from today's verses, fill in these blanks about all that He has done for you.

- He has .... us to share in the inheritance.
- He has .... us from the kingdom of darkness.
- He has .... us into the Kingdom of his dear Son.
- He .... our freedom.
- He .... our sins.

Jesus transferred you to His Kingdom. He rescued you from the grip of the enemy, from the darkness. Live like you belong to His Kingdom now!

Eden

I have been the new kid! When I transferred schools, in all honesty it was hard. I was so scared to enter a new school with all new people and all new teachers and all new everything. I remember crying my eyes out when I transferred in fifth grade.

However, after a week of being in my new school, I started to love it! That was a weird thing for me because I had never even liked school before. Moving was one of the best gifts I have ever received. I quickly made good friends, began to feel at home in my school and church, and the California weather also made me so happy.

I know not everyone loves when they move to a new school, and that is okay. But it's a different story when we become part of God's Kingdom. That is always a great move! Jesus saved us and brought us into His family! We are rescued from our shame, bad choices, fear, and insecurities. We don't live in darkness anymore—we get to live in the light. We can rejoice that Jesus has transferred us to His Kingdom!

Reflection & Discussion Time

- What are a few of the main differences between God's Kingdom and the kingdom of this world?
- From your perspective, what is the best part of being in Jesus' Kingdom?

If anyone is in Christ, the new creation has come: The old has gone, the new is here!

2 CORINTHIANS 5:17, NIV

DAY 34

I Am a New Creation

Eric

If you became a Christian when you were young, you might sometimes feel like your story is boring, especially compared to other people's stories of how Christ changed them. Maybe you have heard some at church, like a guy who met Jesus in prison and now, instead of selling drugs you have never even heard of, he is running an orphanage overseas. Everyone claps and you think, *My story is that I met Jesus at VBS when I was six. Lame!*

But your story is not lame. While the details are different, in the most important way, your story is really the same as the stories that sound so amazing.

You have been made new. There are not levels of new—there is just new. Your old life is gone, and a new life is here! C. S. Lewis wrote that the whole reason God the Son entered our world was to transform people: "God became man to turn creatures into sons: not simply to produce better men of the old kind but to produce a new kind of man."[1]

Jesus did not merely improve the old you. He made a new you.

There is an amazing prophecy in the Old Testament about what God would do for us when He came to our world: "I will give you a new heart, and I will put a new spirit in you. I will take out your stony, stubborn heart and give you a tender, responsive heart" (Ezekiel 36:26). In Scripture, the heart represents the center of who you are. Your whole spiritual life flows from your spiritual heart just as your physical life flows from your physical heart. So to receive a new heart is to become a new person. Your heart was not tweaked or improved. You were given a new heart, and you are a new person!

Because you are a new person, the Scripture commands you to live like you are new: "Put on your new nature, created to be like God—truly righteous and holy" (Ephesians 4:24). You are new, so don't live like your old self anymore!

Eden

I trusted in Jesus and became a Christian when I was very young. I was going into first grade when my dad took me to a church camp where he was speaking. The camp was for third through fifth graders, so everyone felt a lot older. I remember watching the kids and leaders worship with their hands raised, and I wondered why. Later that night, I talked with my dad and asked Jesus to forgive my sins! Like my dad wrote, my story can sound boring. I believed that for years, but once I realized Jesus makes all of us new and not just better people, I was able to walk in confidence with my story. I'm so thankful Jesus saved me as a little girl.

As teens, it is possible our stories aren't super complicated yet. And that is great! We can all walk with confidence in our testimonies because Jesus saved us! We were dead and now we are alive. I love how Ezekiel 36:26 says that he takes out our stony (hard) hearts and gives us tender hearts instead. That is exactly what I want, and it's necessary for all of us whether we have messed up big-time or were saved as a child. We all get a new spirit and a new tender and responsive heart.

Reflection & Discussion Time

- Take a few minutes to write down the story of when you first trusted in Jesus and He made you a new person. Thank Him for all the details of your story, no matter how exciting (or not) it seems to you.
- What changed in your heart and your life once you became a follower of Jesus?

May I never boast except in the cross of our Lord Jesus Christ, through which the world has been crucified to me, and I to the world.

GALATIANS 6:14, NIV

DAY 35

I Am Crucified to the World

Eric

Boasting. You see it all the time. From posts on social media to conversations at school about what someone did or will do or about what someone has or will have. People are savvy, and they will try to boast without looking like they are boasting, but we see it. Often, though, we can see it more easily in others than in ourselves.

The truth is, we can't stop boasting. God created us to boast, to rejoice, to worship, and because He created us to worship, we will all worship and boast in something. Now, God created us to boast in Him, but it's all too easy to find other things to boast in. We can either boast in how great we are, or we can boast in how great Christ is. We can worship Christ, or we can worship something less than Christ. To boast in Christ means to brag about what He has done for us, to rejoice in what He is doing in our lives, to celebrate how awesome He is.

In today's verse, the apostle Paul is praying that he will never boast in anything other than the cross of our Lord Jesus Christ. Boasting in the cross is boasting in Christ because the cross is where we see His character on display. We see both His love and His justice—His love for us and His justice against sin. We see His grace and His wisdom, as He was being gracious to us while also being the One who wisely orchestrated the events to put Himself on the cross. The cross is what Paul rejoices in because it's only through the death of Jesus that we have life. While we may be tempted to boast in something in the world—our accomplishments, our skills, our possessions—Paul says he has been crucified to the world.

What people say about you does not define you; Christ's death for you defines you. Your accomplishments in this world do not define you; what Christ accomplished on the cross for you defines you. Tell others about what He has done, not what you have done.

You can't rid yourself of the desire to rejoice, to celebrate, to boast. God gave you that desire. But because you are a citizen of heaven, transferred to His Kingdom, and a new creation, you can turn your rejoicing to Jesus. Rejoicing in something else won't be enough for you. Only He is enough!

Eden

When I was in kindergarten and first grade, I remember all of the other kids boasting about how many teeth they had lost and how much money the tooth fairy brought them. I was a slow "tooth-loser" and had a stingy tooth fairy. I couldn't boast about either one. But then we started running the mile in PE, and *that* I could boast about—and I did! It feels good to be good at something.

We all have that one friend who is good at whatever they do.

They may even joke that they are bad at something. Which always makes me want to scream because we all know they are actually good! Or maybe you have a friend who always wants to know the grade you made on a test or how many points you made in a game just so they can let you know they did better! I'm not saying this has never been me. I know I have been both of these people. Boasting in ourselves is common, and it can appear in many different forms. It may come from insecurity, pride, jealousy, or some other sin.

We can't get rid of boasting, but according to the passage today, we can redirect our boasting. We can shift boasting about ourselves to boasting in Jesus! It's so easy to get carried away when we boast about ourselves. But if we redirect to boasting in Jesus, we'll be stronger both mentally and spiritually. When I am tempted to boast, I know it's because I have become self-consumed and forgotten the cross.

Reflection & Discussion Time

- Think of a time you boasted about something you did or something you had. What happened? How did you feel afterward—and how did you make others feel?
- What would it look like for you to boast in Jesus at school, church, or home?

Memory Verse

As the Father has sent me, so I am sending you.

JOHN 20:21

WEEK SIX

I Represent Christ

We are Christ's ambassadors; God is making his appeal through us. We speak for Christ when we plead, "Come back to God!" For God made Christ, who never sinned, to be the offering for our sin, so that we could be made right with God through Christ.

2 CORINTHIANS 5:20-21

DAY 36

I Am Christ's Ambassador

Eric

Sometimes I get a direct message on social media asking if I am interested in being an ambassador for a product, if I will post for the brand in exchange for money or some free items. The latest one was offering to send me organic laundry detergent if I would be an ambassador. *Nah.*

In biblical times there were no "brand ambassadors." Ambassadors were sent on a mission from one kingdom to another to represent their king and kingdom in a different land. Still today, our country sends ambassadors to other countries, and other countries send ambassadors here.

You are Christ's ambassador. You are sent to represent Him with a message.

You are sent. In His wisdom, He planned the school you would attend, who would sit next to you in English class, the people alongside you in your extracurricular activities, the neighborhood where you live, all of it. He has placed you in those places on purpose because . . .

You are sent to represent. Ambassadors are not perfect people. They are not in a foreign land to represent themselves but the country they are from. You don't have to be perfect to represent the perfect One who sent you.

You are sent to represent with a message. God makes His appeal to people through you. He delivers His message through you, and that message is that God put all of our sin on Jesus so all His forgiveness would be on us—if we believe in Him. That amazing message has been entrusted to you as His ambassador.

Eden

At my school, we have "student ambassadors." These students try to convince potential students and their parents to choose my high school. They talk highly about our school and share the many opportunities it offers. It was the same when I toured colleges. The tour guides loved the school they attended and would talk highly about it.

We are ambassadors for Christ. We represent Him at our schools, on our teams, and in our friend groups. Once the head of my school said, "Please be careful with what you post on social media because you represent our school." If it's important that I represent my school well, how much more important is the way I represent Jesus? As we represent Him, we are to speak highly of Him and His message.

It's really crazy to think that He puts people in our lives for a purpose. God moves us to certain places, schools, and sports teams for a specific reason. There have been so many times in my life that I have not liked the situation I am in. But when I look back at my life, I see He was using it all for His glory and my good. My club volleyball team my freshman year was a major challenge for many reasons including the fact that I was placed on a very good team as a fairly new volleyball player. My family doesn't quit things, so I asked Jesus to please show me why He had placed me on this team when I could have been on a hundred different teams. And He did. It was my teammates! That season I became close to several girls who are still super important in my life. Jesus allowed me to share my faith with them, and even to this day I see Him working in their lives. That team, while hard, was never a mistake.

We must make the most of where Jesus has placed us. Even as a teen, we are sent on mission for Jesus. We have the responsibility to be ambassadors for Christ.

Reflection & Discussion Time

- Where has Christ sent you to represent Him?
- What can you do this week to represent Him well to others?

Thank God! He has made us his captives and continues to lead us along in Christ's triumphal procession. Now he uses us to spread the knowledge of Christ everywhere, like a sweet perfume. Our lives are a Christ-like fragrance rising up to God. But this fragrance is perceived differently by those who are being saved and by those who are perishing.

2 CORINTHIANS 2:14-15

DAY 37

I Am His Captive and Fragrance

Eric

You have to know a bit of history to appreciate the awesomeness of the above passage. The apostle Paul penned those words during a time in history when the Roman Empire was expanding by taking over cities and lands. Whenever they conquered a group of people, the Roman leaders would march back into Rome in a "triumphal procession" with people they had captured walking behind them. The captives were given the humiliating task of spreading incense as they marched. Not only were they captives, but they were used to help their captors celebrate. It was a sad and traumatic picture—the Roman Empire conquering people and using them in a celebration.

The apostle Paul turns this image upside down and makes it good. He is saying we have been conquered. We belong to His Kingdom now. Christ conquered us, transforming our hearts of stone into new hearts.

A fair question you may have is this: *Wait, I thought I was free in Christ. How can I be free and conquered at the same time?*

You are free from this world and conquered by Christ. Freedom from this world is for your good because this world cannot satisfy you. Though the pressures and struggles of being a teenager can feel overwhelming, the world won't overwhelm you because Christ has freed you. And you have been conquered by Christ, which is also good because Christ ruling your life is much better than you ruling your own life.

The passage also says our lives are like the fragrance of Christ. Because Christ has conquered you, your life is different, so much so that your life "smells like Christ." Now, clearly this is an illustration. We are not talking about an actual, physical scent! It means your life stands out. The Scripture is raw and honest with you about what it means to stand out. Some people will love this about you, but some will not because "this fragrance is perceived differently by those who are being saved and by those who are perishing" (verse 15).

Eden

We all know that one person who has a really strong smell. The minute they walk into a room, everyone knows. Occasionally someone tells me I smell good, and I love that! I don't really have a perfume, but I do wash my hair with scented shampoo! I'm sure not everyone thinks my hair smells good, but that's okay because I do.

As Christians, our scent should be so potent that people will know us by our "Jesus smell." The room should change when we walk in. There should be more joy and hope because of the joy and hope we have in Jesus. Have you ever met someone and thought, *I bet they are a Christian*? You don't know their heart, but you can "smell" them. That sounds weird, but it is what Jesus told us to be—a fragrance for Him.

We are His captives, and He has authority over our lives. Because of this, we should represent Him in all we do! Our smell should be so potent that it rubs off on others around us. As a teen this can be scary because, like 2 Corinthians 2:15 says, not everyone will love our "smell." But if we are willing to be uncomfortable for Him, the reward is so great!

Reflection & Discussion Time

- How would you describe the "Jesus smell" in your life and in the lives of Christians you know?
- What in your life gets in the way of or detracts from the "Jesus smell"?

You will receive power when the Holy Spirit comes upon you. And you will be my witnesses, telling people about me everywhere—in Jerusalem, throughout Judea, in Samaria, and to the ends of the earth.

ACTS 1:8

DAY 38

I Am His Witness

Eric

If you feel unqualified to be a witness, a representative, for Jesus, you are not alone. Most of us feel unqualified. In fact, believing you are unqualified in your own power is what qualifies you to depend on His power!

After Jesus rose from the dead and before He ascended back into heaven, Jesus told His disciples, "You *will be* my witnesses." He did not say, "You might be." He also did not say, "You will go witnessing." Witnessing is something you do. Jesus is speaking about who His disciples will *be*. The reason Jesus was so confident that His disciples would be His witnesses and change the world was not because He was confident in them. Jesus had seen all but one of them scatter in fear when He went to the cross. Jesus knew they struggled in their own strength. The disciples were also really young—most of them were teenagers or young adults at the time. They were not seasoned or mature.

So why was Jesus so confident these disciples would take the news about Jesus all over the world, beginning where they lived in Jerusalem? Because Jesus had promised them the Holy Spirit. They had walked next to God when they walked next to Jesus, but now God was going to move into their lives. The Spirit empowered them to tell people about Jesus, to start churches, to serve others, and to turn the world upside down. The Christian faith spread like crazy because of God's extraordinary power through some ordinary teenagers.

God still changes the world that way—with ordinary people who feel unqualified but rely on His power. God has always been on a mission to bring people to Himself, and God moved into your life when you became a Christian. What qualifies you to be His witness is not your intelligence or your people skills or anything else like that. The Spirit was sent to you to equip you to share God's love with others.

Eden

I never really got into the Marvel movies or superheroes, but many of my friends did. From what I know, superheroes are usually just ordinary people who suddenly receive powers and gifts that make them capable of doing extraordinary things to save the world.

As Christians, our superpower is the Holy Spirit! We are able to do hard, bold things because the Holy Spirit empowers us. As a matter of fact, anything good we do is because of Him. The Holy Spirit even empowers us to tell others about God's work in our lives.

Does anyone else think trying new things is scary? Continuing in what I am good at and comfortable in sounds great, but I know from experience that's not when I grow. Jesus is so good to us to give us the Holy Spirit to be with us as we serve Him. That means even when I do hard things, I am never alone.

I am so grateful that He has chosen to use me, because I know He doesn't need me. In the fall of 2023, God put a desire on the hearts of me and my friend Kamryn to start a nonprofit for teens with disabilities (Love Without Limits). We really had no idea what we were doing! I had a lot of concerns and was super unsure of myself, but He kept leading. He has empowered me to lead volunteers, plan and execute each event, and share my passion for special needs with others. I would never have been able to do any of this on my own. I didn't have the knowledge, confidence, or strength. Only because of the guidance of the Holy Spirit has Love Without Limits continued to grow and show His love to many families.

Reflection & Discussion Time

- Think of a time you tried something new. What was that experience like? What did you learn from it?
- How does knowing you can rely on God's power change your view of going outside your comfort zone to serve Him?

As the Father has sent me, so I am sending you.

JOHN 20:21

DAY 39

I Am Sent

Eric

You have likely heard of the biblical account of Jonah and the big fish. The story does not begin with the fish swallowing Jonah, but with Jonah being sent by God:

> The LORD gave this message to Jonah: "Get up and go to the great city of Nineveh. Announce my judgment against it because I have seen how wicked its people are."
> JONAH 1:1-2

Jonah ran from God, boarded a ship, and went the exact opposite direction from Nineveh. God sent a storm, people threw Jonah overboard, and that is when the fish enters the story. God was not punishing Jonah; God was pursuing Jonah—wanting Jonah to obey Him and be part of His plan. After Jonah is swallowed and then spit out by the large fish, we read this:

> Then the LORD spoke to Jonah a second time: "Get up and go to the great city of Nineveh, and deliver the message I have given you." This time Jonah obeyed the LORD's command and went to Nineveh.
>
> JONAH 3:1-3

Look at the first few verses of Jonah 1 and 3. What is the same and what is different?

Same command. Different response. I guess three days in the belly of a large fish will do that to you! Side note: People sometimes think it is odd that I believe the story of Jonah and the fish to be true. My answer is, "That is not even the craziest thing I believe. I believe Jesus is God and walked out of the tomb, and because I believe that, I believe all Jesus said, and Jesus talked about Jonah!"

Okay, back to the main point of today . . . A great revival spread throughout the city of Nineveh, not because of Jonah's powerful speaking but because God's Word is always sufficient. The Scripture says that people repented in Nineveh "from the greatest to the least" (Jonah 3:5). The same message impacted poets and plumbers, leaders and laborers. *All people* need God's message.

Jonah was sent by God to the city of Nineveh not because God needed Jonah but because God wanted to work in Jonah's life and in the lives of the people in Nineveh. God sends you not because He needs you but because you need His mission. As you step out of your comfort zone, you are changed. Jesus told His disciples that just as He was sent, He was sending them (see John 20:21). Jesus was sent to this world to serve you and to rescue you, and He has sent you to serve others and to share God's message of rescue.

Eden

I love what my dad said above: God sends us not because He needs us, but because we need His mission. When I think back over my sophomore year in high school, sometimes it looks like a mess. There were many ups and downs of all kinds. I made a lot of good decisions and a lot of dumb decisions. However, I can now see God's hand in it all. Recently my mom and I listed all the ways I can now see God at work throughout that year. Looking back, I can see He was chasing me and pursuing me—but I was running, and I didn't know it.

In March of my sophomore year, I went on a mission trip to Uganda. On that trip, I saw Jesus and was never the same afterward. Shortly after returning from that trip, I took a class on how to study the Bible. (My mom actually taught it, so it was kind of mandatory!) My friend Abie, who went on the Uganda trip with me and was also part of the Bible class, approached me and said, "We should start a Bible study for juniors and seniors who want to go deeper and study the Bible."

I was like, "Okay! It'll be fun to make new friends."

He kind of looked at me like I was missing the point. Even though I'd said yes, I was so nervous about starting this. I mean, would anyone actually come to my house on a Friday night to sit and talk about the Bible? I kept pushing out the date of the first meeting. Thankfully Abie is pretty persistent, in the best way, and finally we just did it. Throughout the summer, we watched Jesus work. He established a leadership team of people I truly admire and love serving with, He drew us closer to Him, and He gave us a desire for His Word. The Lord brought more juniors and seniors from more high schools than we could have imagined. The study that we thought would last just through the summer is still going strong into my junior year. I'm so glad Jesus didn't let me say no. He didn't need me, but I sure needed this.

Reflection & Discussion Time

- How would you view your day tomorrow differently if you believed you were sent by God to all the places you go?
- Think of a time you obeyed God, even when it was hard. What happened? How did you see Him at work?

Go and make disciples of all the nations, baptizing them in the name of the Father and the Son and the Holy Spirit. Teach these new disciples to obey all the commands I have given you. And be sure of this: I am with you always, even to the end of the age.

MATTHEW 28:19-20

DAY 40

I Am Commissioned

Eric

You learned in history class that Thomas Jefferson served as our nation's third president and was the principal author of the Declaration of Independence. For that I am thankful. What many don't know is that Thomas Jefferson took a penknife and removed sections of the Gospels he did not think to be true or relevant to him. He cut out all the miracles of Jesus and titled his version *The Life and Morals of Jesus of Nazareth*, but the work is commonly called the Jefferson Bible. Dude made his own Bible! You can buy it on Amazon. And in it, there is no virgin birth, no resurrection from the dead, and no great commission. Most Christians think, *No way I would cut passages out of the Bible like that.* But if we ignore them, isn't that the same thing?

Matthew 28:19-20 is known as the great commission because Jesus, who has all authority over everything, commissioned His followers to make disciples of all nations. Just as God gave authority to Adam and Eve to be fruitful and multiply, God gave authority to His disciples to multiply. You have been given authority too. You are commissioned.

Jesus reminded His disciples that as they go, He will always be with them. He is with you always too because His Spirit lives within you. But the more you obey this command, the more you will know He is with you. The more you embrace helping other people follow Jesus, the more you will be aware of His presence.

Notice part of the great commission is to make disciples "of all the nations." The word for "nations" in the original language refers to people groups. God is bringing sons and daughters into His family from every single people group. Heaven will be full of people from all over the world. We see this when we get to the end of the Bible and read about Jesus receiving worship in heaven: "You are worthy to take the scroll and break its seals and open it. For you were slaughtered, and your blood has ransomed people for God from every tribe and language and people and nation" (Revelation 5:9). God has chosen us to be the means by which this happens.

Don't cut this out of your Bible! Don't miss the joy of being a global Christian because our God is for people from all over the globe. Yes, make disciples where you are. But also start looking for ways to participate in making disciples of all nations. Maybe participating in a mission trip? Maybe giving to global outreach at your church or praying for missionaries?

Eden

I love mission trips sooooo much! I know not everyone has the opportunity, but if you do, go! It's so cool to explore the world and get to know new people. It always surprises me how similar I am to kids across the globe. We have much more in common than we think. My favorite part about mission trips though is seeing God move. It happens every single time. He not only moves in those places, but He moves in my heart without fail.

To serve people who are different than us requires getting out of our comfort zone. This means the possibility of making a mistake is great, and as I've mentioned before, I don't like to make mistakes.

My parents decided that we would try our best to go on a mission trip as a family every year starting when I was in sixth grade and my sister, Evie, was in fourth. In the beginning I was so uncomfortable and nervous. The unknown freaked me out. Our first trip was to Haiti, and it was not easy. It was hot, there were huge mosquitoes, and we were in a poverty-stricken area. However, meeting and getting to know the people in that community was truly life-changing for me and encouraging for them. Still today, I experience some fear going into every mission trip, but God uses my discomfort to help me grow in Him.

On the trip, one of our group leaders encouraged us that God did not want to send us around the world only to have us come back the same. And I have never come home the same. Not one time. There is so much power within the global church, and it's a gift when we get to connect with each other.

Reflection & Discussion Time

- Have you ever been tempted to "cut out" or ignore part of God's Word? What about that part of the Bible did you object to?
- Brainstorm some ways you can participate in God's global work. Could you learn more about Christians in other cultures? Could you support or pray for missionaries from your church? Could you go on a mission trip? Ask a parent or pastor for ideas of how to get involved.

You are the salt of the earth. But what good is salt if it has lost its flavor? Can you make it salty again? It will be thrown out and trampled underfoot as worthless.

MATTHEW 5:13

DAY 41

I Am the Salt of the Earth

Eric

Today when someone says, "You're salty," they typically mean you are expressing yourself with an edge, with some bitterness or frustration. This is *not* what Jesus meant when He told His followers that they were "the salt of the earth."

Refrigerators and freezers didn't exist back in the days when Jesus and His disciples walked the earth, so people used salt to preserve food from decaying. But like today, salt was also used to add flavor to food. So when Jesus called His followers the salt of the earth, He was telling them that because they belong to Jesus' Kingdom, they preserve and add flavor wherever they go.

If you follow Jesus, you, too, are the salt of the earth. You preserve and you add flavor.

Without God's grace, everything decays. A society, a school, a neighborhood, a team, a city will decay without God's presence. Unless there is salt present, people will be taken advantage of, the poor will be neglected, people created in God's image will be mistreated, and hatred will increase. You often don't think you are making a difference, but wherever you are, if you are living as a citizen of God's Kingdom, your presence is preventing decay.

As salt, you also add flavor. Jesus called His disciples salt because they brought the flavor of God's Kingdom: they were poor and humble in spirit, hungering for God's righteousness, merciful, pure in their hearts toward God, and peaceful (see Matthew 5:1-8). They had been changed by Jesus, and they would change the world. Changed people change the world.

As you live the values of Jesus' Kingdom, your presence makes your school, your team, and your community taste better. Your attitude of humility inspires people. Your joy because Jesus has made you His child encourages people. Your mercy toward those who are mistreated or picked on encourages kindness toward others. Your desire for peace rather than gossip, backbiting, hatred, or bitterness makes everywhere you go better. Keep showing up in all the places God puts you as someone who has been changed by Jesus, and you will be making a bigger difference than you know. You are the salt of the earth, and that is what salt does!

Eden

I love salt. Honestly, it is the best thing ever. Someone once asked me if I could have any seasoning or sauce come out of my elbow, what would I choose? I obviously answered salt. I think it is so cool that Jesus calls us the salt of the earth. We are called to flavor and preserve the atmosphere around us!

You know that one friend who lights up every room they walk into, the one who brings so much "flavor"? When that person is gone, the whole group dynamic is thrown off. As Christians, we are this very salt whether we realize it or not. As teens, we can be salt in our community, school, sports teams, friend groups, and even with our family. We flavor our community by our actions and words.

We get to bring something that no one else can. Jesus has given us different gifts to sharpen each other and serve the people around us. Where Jesus isn't present, life will not last. But because the Holy Spirit lives inside of us, our presence can guide others in the right direction, and our values can help us make sound decisions.

It can be hard to live by our convictions. Because when it comes down to it, convenience is easier than conviction. To stand strong in a group and not fall into temptation is hard but so important. We are the salt when we stay true to our faith. Being salt is not a small role—it's a huge honor!

Reflection & Discussion Time

- Where is your presence making an impact as "the salt of the earth"?
- Who is someone you respect who holds to his or her convictions? What do you think it takes to stay committed to your convictions?

You are the light of the world—like a city on a hilltop that cannot be hidden. No one lights a lamp and then puts it under a basket. Instead, a lamp is placed on a stand, where it gives light to everyone in the house. In the same way, let your good deeds shine out for all to see, so that everyone will praise your heavenly Father.

MATTHEW 5:14-16

DAY 42

I Am the Light of the World

Eric

Immediately after telling His disciples that they were "the salt of the earth," He told them they were "the light of the world." What makes this declaration so stunning is that Jesus alsc declared Himself to be the light of the world:

> I am the light of the world. If you follow me, you won't have to walk in darkness, because you will have the light that leads to life.
>
> JOHN 8:12

It is one of the seven "I Am" statements we find in the Gospel of John, where Jesus claims to be God. Jesus did not merely make big statements; He always backed them up with actions. When He said, "I am the resurrection and the life" (John 11:25), He raised a dead man to life. When He said, "I am the bread of life" (John 6:35), He fed five thousand people with two fish and five loaves of bread. Right after saying, "I am the light of the world" (John 9:5), Jesus put light in a blind man's eyes.

But Jesus also calls His people the light of the world and commands us not to hide our light. When Jesus walked this earth, there was no electricity, so people lit their homes with oil lamps. These were not merely decorations like the lamps of today—they were an important source of light in homes at night. But a lamp was useless if it was hidden under a basket. The whole point of the lamp was to help everyone see. God wants you to live in a way so that everyone sees by your light. Read the passage again. What does Jesus say should shine in your life? What will people see in your life?

The way to live your identity as the light of the world is through your good deeds. The way you serve people, the way you love, the way you forgive, the way you are willing to be made fun of because you stand out, the way you hunger for God more than the things of this world. You are the light of the world, and your good deeds matter! How you talk to your teachers and about your teachers matters. How you treat people at school matters. How you talk, how you react, how you spend time on the weekends, how you use social media—all of it matters because you are the light of the world!

Eden

When I was little, I could only sleep if I had a night-light. I was scared of the dark because I thought a monster would come after me. Now, I love the dark. I can only sleep when it's dark, and I love to sleep. Every morning when my mom wakes me up (I can wake myself up, but for some reason she likes to do this!), I beg her not to turn the light on. I know as soon as the light comes on, my sleep is over. Light changes things; it has a lot of power. When light comes, darkness disappears.

Jesus calls Himself the "light of the world." As a Jesus follower, I know this to be true. His presence in my life has changed me. The light won over the darkness of my own soul. He also tells us *we* are the light. Like Jesus, we are to stand out in dark places because we are different.

Sometimes the hardest places are the places you feel like you are the only light. I've been there. It almost seems like there is too much darkness for our little bit of light to overtake. But think about that. When it's really dark and you light one match, the light overtakes the darkness. We are that one match. As the light, we give comfort and help to the people around us. Sometimes people will think we are odd or weird because of our faith. That might make us want to turn down our light, but it means they're noticing the difference in us and wondering about it. The light is doing what light does!

Light spreads through a dark room, and our faith will spread through our actions, through our lives. One of my favorite things we do at my church is the candlelight service at Christmas. It starts with one candle, and before we know it, the once-dark space turns into a beautiful, bright room. As the light of our lives spreads, it influences others and brings people to Jesus.

Reflection & Discussion Time

- When are you most tempted to turn down your light as a Christian?
- What are some good deeds you've done (or could do) that help people see Jesus and praise Him?

Memory Verse

I am convinced that neither death nor life, neither angels nor demons, neither the present nor the future, nor any powers, neither height nor depth, nor anything else in all creation, will be able to separate us from the love of God that is in Christ Jesus our Lord.

ROMANS 8:38-39, NIV

WEEK SEVEN

God Is for Me

There is no greater love than to lay down one's life for one's friends. You are my friends if you do what I command. I no longer call you slaves, because a master doesn't confide in his slaves. Now you are my friends, since I have told you everything the Father told me.

JOHN 15:13-15

DAY 43

I Am God's Friend

Eric

We know that Jesus' disciples called themselves servants (see day 25 of this devotional). They embraced the low title of being servants of Jesus because they held such a high view of Him. Being servants of Jesus brought them great joy; it was not a bad thing at all. But in the above passage, as Jesus is preparing to die for His disciples (and for you and me), Jesus looked at them and said, "I am now calling you my friends." Jesus calls you His friend too.

What qualities in someone make a good friend? Go ahead and list them here:

Now look at your list. My hunch is your list is similar to mine with qualities like *loyal*, *encouraging*, *wise*, *caring*, and *joyful*. When I look at my list, I realize that Jesus is the best at all those qualities. No one is loyal like Him—He is with me no matter what. No one is as encouraging as Him. For sure, no one is as wise and caring as He is. He knows everything and has the ability to work things for my good. He brings joy like no one else can.

Read the passage one more time and see what Jesus says He does for His friends. You can fill in these blanks.

- There is no greater love than to ....
....
....
....

- You are my friends if ....
....
....

Jesus is not a silent friend. He shares His Word with you as you read the Bible. He leads you and directs you by His Spirit, who lives within you. And there is no greater love than His love because He willingly laid down His life for you.

Eden

I love people, and I love making new friends. But not everyone is a reliable friend. Since I am always so eager to make new friends, I can get hurt because I fail to realize that not everyone is good for me to be around. Not everyone will treat me the same way I treat them. This can be a hurtful experience. I pride myself on being a good, genuine, loyal friend—and I am for the most part, but I fail too.

Ultimately, Jesus is the best friend we could ever dream of. It's normal to have trouble with friends as a teen. People are maturing at different rates, and our interests seem to change daily. Navigating friendships can be a lot! Sometimes it feels like we have no "true friend." We just feel alone. Thankfully, we are not alone! Someone once told me that when he accepted Jesus, he was dropped by all his friends because his desires changed and he no longer wanted to do the things they had done before. During this time, he leaned on Jesus and found He is the best friend. He's the only one who never leaves or forsakes us, is never too busy to listen, gives perfect wisdom, stands by our side, and comforts us even when we're being dumb.

I have great friends, and I am so thankful for them. Good friends are a gift, but if we put all of our hope in them, we are asking them to be something they can never be. As great as friendships can be, they will never live up to the friendship we have in Jesus. When we invest in our relationship with Jesus, we will never regret it. I pray I can show Jesus to others by the kind of friend I am to them—and point them to Him, the best friend they could ever have.

Reflection & Discussion Time

- How has Jesus been a good friend to you?
- How can you be a good friend to others so they see what Jesus' friendship is like?

As God's partners, we beg you not to accept this marvelous gift of God's kindness and then ignore it.

2 CORINTHIANS 6:1

DAY 44

I Am God's Partner

Eric

A story is told of a mouse who sat on an elephant's back as they crossed a bridge together. When they got to the other side and the bridge was still shaking, the mouse said to the elephant, "We sure shook that bridge, didn't we?" The elephant did not need the mouse to shake the bridge, but the elephant enjoyed partnering with the mouse.

You are God's partner. He has chosen to work with you. Here are two examples of God partnering with people in Scripture with some questions for you to consider:

> **Example 1:** After God created everything, He brought the animals to Adam "to see what he would call them, and the man chose a name for each one" (Genesis 2:19). God created this beautiful earth and everything in it, and He then gave Adam the freedom of naming the animals.

Surely God was not out of energy or in need of Adam's help. Why do you think God asked Adam to name the animals?

Example 2: When Jesus fed five thousand people, He asked Philip where they could buy bread not because He did not know what He was going to do but because "he already knew what he was going to do" (John 6:6). Andrew found a boy who had two fish and five small loaves of bread, and Jesus turned the kid's lunch-box-size meal into enough food to feed the entire crowd. The disciples passed out the food and collected the leftovers—just enough for them to eat too. Why do you think Jesus included His disciples in this miracle?

God the Father did not need Adam, but He loved working with Adam to name the animals. God the Son, Jesus, did not need to include the disciples, but He loved involving them. Because God loves you, He loves to partner with you to serve people, to do great work in the world, and to make an impact on others. Because God loves you, He loves working with you. You have God as your study partner. You have God as your teammate. You have God as your partner in all you will do in life.

God will do powerful work in your life, and you get to be partners with Him.

Eden

All right, guys, I'm going to bring up the crush thing again. Let's be real, when we like someone, we do some crazy things. Like, have you ever asked your crush for help on homework that you totally know how to do? I definitely have. I've seen other people doing it too. We look for any opportunity to "talk."

Jesus does something similar with us! He doesn't have a romantic crush on us, but He does love to be with us. He chooses to partner with us not because He needs us, but because He loves us. He wants to do life with us and use us in His plan! I remember the first time I heard He was jealous for me, and I thought, *That doesn't make sense. It's wrong to be jealous.* Once I came to understand that He is jealous for my affections, my time, and my attention, it made sense. He loves me too much to let anything else steal all of that.

As teens, we can be His partners. He doesn't just use adults—He also uses teens. He cares for all of His children and loves to work with us and through us. So next time I'm scared, I can remind myself that Jesus is partnering with me. Any time I'm confused about the next chapter of my life or why something occurred, I can remind myself that His plan is better than anything I could come up with. He is using me, and He wants me to enjoy life with Him too.

Reflection & Discussion Time

- Where in your life do you think God wants to partner with you? If you're not sure, ask Him to make it clear to you!
- What does it mean to you that God wants to work with you but does not need you?

Before you Gentiles knew God, you were slaves to so-called gods that do not even exist. So now that you know God (or should I say, now that God knows you), why do you want to go back again and become slaves once more to the weak and useless spiritual principles of this world?

GALATIANS 4:8-9

DAY 45

I Am Known by God

Eric

God knows you! He knows all there is to know about you. He knows the number of hairs on your head, your favorite subject in school, your favorite foods, and the shoes that you love. He not only knows about you, though; He knows *you*. Meaning He understands you. He gets your personality. He knows your struggles and your hopes.

He knows you even better than the closest friends you have ever had. In fact, He knows you better than you know yourself. There are some things you may keep from your friends because you worry it would push them away. But God knows everything about you, and He loves you. The God who created everything you see and experience has decided to know you personally. He treats you as His friend.

The psalmist marveled over this—that the God who painted the sky with His finger wanted to know him. He wrote:

> When I look at the night sky and see the work of your
> fingers—
> the moon and the stars you set in place—
> what are mere mortals that you should think about them,
> human beings that you should care for them?
>
> PSALM 8:3-4

Because God knows you, it is foolish to worship something or someone other than Him—what Paul refers to in Galatians 4:8 as "so-called gods." The little-*g* gods of this world don't know you and can't know you because only God is your Creator and Savior.

Knowing you are known by God is a game-changer for your life. It will change the way you pray, the way you worship, and even your confidence as you know He always has your back and is always with you and for you.

Eden

Any time I get in trouble with my parents (normally it's for fighting with my sister about clothes), I usually say, "You don't understand." I think that's a fair statement, since they were not there for the argument! Maybe sometimes you feel like your parents or friends don't understand you. In a way this is true. No one but Jesus can fully read our minds and hearts, including us!

After every argument that my sister, Evie, thinks ends unfairly, she will say, "Eden, God knows your heart." She tries to make it clear that God knows if I'm being sincere in my apology or explanation to our parents. Although *her* heart may not be right making this statement, Evie is correct. Only God truly knows my heart.

As teens, we often feel like we have to put on a persona to fit in or act a certain way to please people. But with God we don't have to do that. We can go to Him just as we are. He doesn't want us to hide anything—He wants us to come open and honest. We can tell Him what we are struggling with, our doubts, and all our questions. He won't condemn us; He will receive us with kindness and grace.

Jesus wants to talk to us and wants the real version of us. He does not want us to act fake in order to look good. He knows everything about us. He knows even more than we know about ourselves. We can talk to Him openly because He knows what we are thinking even before we do. If we don't go to Him authentically in prayer, we can miss what He wants to say to us, what He wants to show us. Jesus tells us to come as we are, but if we do, we won't stay that way. The more we spend time with Jesus, the more we will change because He changes us.

Reflection & Discussion Time

- What is challenging or scary about God knowing everything about you?
- What is comforting about God knowing everything about you?

Since God chose you to be the holy people he loves, you must clothe yourselves with tenderhearted mercy, kindness, humility, gentleness, and patience.

COLOSSIANS 3:12

DAY 46

I Am Deeply Loved

Eric

We live in a world that loves us based on how we look or what we do—not based on who we are. Think about how the world works:

- Play really well on the team, win a championship, and then we will love you as a hero.
- Make great grades, participate in lots of extracurricular activities, and then we would love to have you attend our university.
- Look and act a certain way, and then we would love to have you in our friend group.

The list could go on and on.

The reason we have a difficult time believing that God loves us just because He is love is that His love is so different from the world's. It also can bother us a bit if we're honest because we like to think we have done something to earn His love. But notice the order in today's verse and how different God's love toward you is.

Fill in the blanks below:

- Since God chose you to be ....
...., you must . . .

If God loved you the way the world does, the verse would read like this: "Clothe yourselves with mercy, kindness, and humility, and then God will love you." Do you see how different God's love is? He wants you to obey Him not so that He will love you but because He already does.

Because He loves you, you must live like He does, and that means it's time to wear some new clothes. Not clothes you get at the mall—clothes that really make you stand out, that last and make an impact on others. These are the clothes of mercy, kindness, humility, gentleness, and patience. You have to decide to wear those each day, to put them on. It's not always easy because putting these things on means going against the current or rhythm of this world. But you are able to clothe yourself with mercy, kindness, humility, gentleness, and patience because you have received the otherworldly love of God and His love motivates you and keeps changing you!

Eden

Earning someone's love is something we see on every social media platform and throughout daily life. I can think of so many movies where the girl feels like she has to change herself to be liked. I think of that kid who feels that he needs to change to be loved by his parents. Or maybe we think, *I will only be popular and liked if I'm a better athlete.* The list goes on and on. It's so easy to believe this is true because of what the world tells us.

God's attitude toward us could not be more different! Today's verse says that God chose me. He chose me because He loves me. He didn't choose because I'm a great athlete or because I'm pretty. He loves me because He loves me. The world can beat us up as teens. It is honestly really hard to even believe someone could love and choose me just because they love me. It's also a daily battle to remember this and respond to situations with this in mind.

Sometimes I just don't want to be kind and gentle to someone who has hurt me. But God is kind and gentle, and He invites me to be the same way. My parents often remind my sister and me of this. When we struggle to respond in a Christlike way, it's because we have forgotten what He has done for us. This is true! If I struggle to show mercy, kindness, humility, gentleness, and patience, it's because I have forgotten how freely God shows these to me daily. These are not my natural responses in my own skin. But because of the Holy Spirit I can put on my new clothes!

Reflection & Discussion Time

- Which of these new clothes do you find the most challenging to wear: mercy, kindness, humility, gentleness, or patience? Why is that one hard?
- Is it difficult for you to believe that you don't have to do anything to earn God's love? Why or why not?

Since you have been raised to new life with Christ, set your sights on the realities of heaven, where Christ sits in the place of honor at God's right hand. Think about the things of heaven, not the things of earth. For you died to this life, and your real life is hidden with Christ in God. And when Christ, who is your life, is revealed to the whole world, you will share in all his glory.

COLOSSIANS 3:1-4

DAY 47

I Am with Christ

Eric

"Are you with me?"

"For sure, I am with you."

Maybe you have had that type of conversation with a friend, where you want to be sure your friend is in agreement about a decision or some activity you plan to do together. You really hope your friend will say, "I am with you in this."

When Jesus entered this world, the angel announced that Jesus is Immanuel—which means "God with us" (Matthew 1:23, NIV). Jesus is so committed to being with you that He left heaven and entered this world to live perfectly and die on your behalf—and then to enter your life. He is the best at being with you.

Look at the amazing passage above. Underline every time you see the phrase "with Christ." Then answer these questions:

- Which part of the passage is about your old life?

- Which part is about life right now?

- Which part is about eternal life?

When you became a Christian, you died *with* Christ. That means all of your sin and shame died. As Christ died on the cross, your old life died with Him. And just as Christ rose from the dead, you have a new life *with* Jesus. Your new life—your real life—is hidden *with* Christ! When I was a kid playing hide-and-go-seek in teams, I always wanted to hide with the person who knew all the great spots. As a Christian, you are hidden with Christ. The enemy and the world will not be able to take you from Him. Just as Christ lives forever, you will live forever *with* Him, appearing *with* Him in glory!

You are never alone. More than anyone else is with you or will ever be with you, Jesus is with you.

Eden

I don't like to be alone in a crowd. Have you ever noticed girls go to the bathroom in packs? Actually, we do everything in groups! It's comforting to know that we have each other. Occasionally, I do have to suck it up and walk into an unfamiliar place without my friends. And I don't love it when I have to do it alone.

Thankfully, Jesus is always with me. Remembering this is a huge comfort. He is unlike any other person in my life because He never changes. When I wander away, He is still faithful to me. When I am a brat, He is still there. He's never too busy or uninterested in my silly concerns (and I do have those!). It's amazing that not only did He love and pursue me first, but then in my brokenness He chose to save me. And He promises to stay with me! He lets me get to know Him through His Word, worship, and prayer.

I love the part of this passage from Colossians that says, "your real life is hidden with Christ in God." My old life is gone. It is dead. Sometimes I try to bring it back, but Jesus reminds me that His death covered that sinful life. I looked up the word *hidden*, and it means "being out of sight" or "concealed."[1] My real life is safe with Jesus. No matter how many times I mess up, fail, or forget who I am in Him, my real life is secure.

Reflection & Discussion Time

- What is your response to the fact that God loves to be with you?
- What are some ways you could get to know God better?

Those God foreknew he also predestined to be conformed to the image of his Son.

ROMANS 8:29, NIV

I am certain that God, who began the good work within you, will continue his work until it is finally finished on the day when Christ Jesus returns.

PHILIPPIANS 1:6

DAY 48

I Am Being Conformed

Eric

You have likely heard a teacher, a parent, or a counselor drop a cliché on you about the importance of choosing friends wisely—a cliché like "Show me your friends, and I will show you your future." Lines like that can sound cheesy, but the reason they are often repeated is because your friends do matter a ton. They impact who you are becoming. You often conform your beliefs and your behaviors to those of your closest friends.

Jesus has made you His friend. The more you spend time with Him, the more you become like Him—which is for your good. The more you become like Him, the more joyful you become, the more holy you become, and the greater impact you will have on this world.

Take another look at today's verses. God did not only save you and forgive you, He planned to conform you to the image of Jesus—to change you. When you became a Christian, God began this good work in you, but He is not finished. He is working on you now, and He will not stop until—read Philippians 1:6 again. When will God be finished working on you?

Imagine how much you would have to love something to be committed to working on it for years and years. He is so committed to changing you that He won't stop until Christ returns to make everything new and right in the world. That is serious commitment. He is your eternal friend, and He will never back away from you.

Eden

I remember praying for friends before we moved to California. I was about to enter fifth grade and was leaving behind a street full of friends with whom I played every single day. We knew each other so well, we were almost more like sisters than friends. Jesus was so good to me, as He had sister-friends waiting for me in California too. These friends have been instrumental in shaping who I am, what I believe, and what I aspire to be. They have made me better, and I am deeply grateful.

If spending time with wonderful friends can change me, how much more life-altering must spending time with Jesus be? There are times when I am slow to spend time with Him because I feel unworthy. However, today's verses remind me that it has always been His plan to shape me. He has never expected me to be the perfect friend to Him that He is to me. He knew when He saved me that I would need a lot of work, and He has been incredibly kind in drawing me to Himself.

I have loved worship music for a long time and have always seen it as a way to connect with Jesus. However, I desperately wanted to develop a love for reading my Bible. I heard my parents speak about their love for the Bible, and while I would read it, I didn't share that love. My mom told me that all I needed was the desire and that if I read consistently, Jesus would do the rest. And He did! I'm not sure exactly when or how, but He began to give me a love for His Word and excitement to read it. The more I read, the more I felt convicted about parts of my life that didn't align with who He is. I'm still not as consistent as I would like to be, but I'm so grateful that He is more patient and kind to me than I could ever imagine, and that He never gives up on making me more like Him.

Reflection & Discussion Time

- What areas of your life has God changed? How were those areas different before they changed?
- Where do you believe God is working in your life right now?

If God is for us, who can be against us? He who did not spare his own Son, but gave him up for us all—how will he not also, along with him, graciously give us all things? Who will bring any charge against those whom God has chosen? It is God who justifies. Who then is the one who condemns? No one. Christ Jesus who died—more than that, who was raised to life—is at the right hand of God and is also interceding for us. Who shall separate us from the love of Christ? Shall trouble or hardship or persecution or famine or nakedness or danger or sword? . . . No, in all these things we are more than conquerors through him who loved us. For I am convinced that neither death nor life, neither angels nor demons, neither the present nor the future, nor any powers, neither height nor depth, nor anything else in all creation, will be able to separate us from the love of God that is in Christ Jesus our Lord.

ROMANS 8:31-35, 37-39, NIV

DAY 49

I Am More than a Conqueror

Eric

Some questions are not really questions but statements masked as questions—also known as rhetorical questions. For example, when my wife asks me, "Are you going to wear that?" it's not truly a question. She is actually saying, "Please don't wear that. You don't match. You should change."

As we get to the end of this devotional, we are going to look at five amazing rhetorical questions in the passage above. Like my wife asking if I am "going to wear that," these aren't really questions. They're statements of God's great commitment to you and love for you.

I am really proud of you for spending this much time in the Bible. I hope you feel more confident in your faith and how to grow closer to Jesus. Life is challenging, and the above passage will help you remember that your friendship with Jesus is never going to end—that He is going to stay committed to you, that His love for you endures. This makes you more than a conqueror because no struggles or challenges in this life can take you away from His love. The questions in Romans 8:31-39 profoundly confront the doubts we may have about God's love.

1. If God is for us, who can be ....?

Of course, people are against you at times, but they are not nearly as strong as God, so they will not be able to overcome you.

2. How will He not also, along with Him, ... us all things?

God gave up His Son, Jesus, for you. Anything else He could give you is insignificant by comparison, so of course He is going to keep being generous to you!

3. Who will bring any charge against those whom God has chosen? It is God ....

The voice of your enemy, Satan, is silenced by God's loud and powerful voice because you have been justified! (Look back at days 15 and 16.)

4. Who then is the one who condemns? No one. Christ Jesus who died—more than that, who was raised to life—is at the right hand of God and is also ....

Jesus died for you, was raised for you, and is praying for you now. (Look back at day 30.)

5. Who shall separate us from the love of Christ? . . . No, in all these things we are ....

....

You will never be separated from your friendship with Christ because He conquered death for you, and He will conquer anything that could separate you from Him.

Eden

Do you remember a time when you felt there was no way you could overcome the challenges before you? No chance of success? When I was six, I was diagnosed with PANDAS (Pediatric Autoimmune Neuropsychiatric Disorders Associated with Streptococcal Infections). Essentially, this means that a strep infection traveled to my brain and caused me to act abnormally. I remember feeling strange and experiencing sudden fears that I couldn't explain, and my parents were confused. They tried to love, comfort, and talk with me, but nothing seemed to work until they found a doctor who understood PANDAS and knew how to treat it. He had the answers we had been searching for. Through his medical care and Jesus' help, PANDAS did not win, and I was healed.

There have been times in my life when winning a battle felt unlikely. I have felt defeated, unworthy, and insecure. I've experienced loneliness, fear, judgment, anxiety, and I've felt like I was in a deep hole. On my own, I lacked the strength and weapons to fight these battles. Yet Jesus graciously reminds me that His power is made perfect in my weakness (see 2 Corinthians 12:9). I am a conqueror because of who He is in me and because He fights for me. When I feel that people or circumstances are against me, I remind myself that He is for me. When I remember His purpose in me, I remember that He will provide everything I need.

I already have the greatest gift—Jesus. When the enemy attacks and his voice seems the loudest, I remember that Jesus has already defeated Satan. When I feel condemned, I remind myself that I live to please only Jesus (though this can be challenging!). In moments of defeat, I remember that I am a conqueror *in Him*. Thank You, Jesus!

Reflection & Discussion Time

- Which of the five questions in Romans 8:31-39 is most encouraging to you? Why?
- What is a challenge in your life that Jesus has helped you overcome?

You are a chosen people. You are royal priests, a holy nation, God's very own possession. As a result, you can show others the goodness of God, for he called you out of the darkness into his wonderful light.

1 PETER 2:9

DAY 50

I Am . . . So That

As we have seen over these fifty days together, God has a lot to say about understanding and embracing who you are. A lot to say about your identity. Today's verse reminds us that He has given us a new identity not only for our own benefit but so we can show others the goodness of God.

As you conclude this devotional, take some time over the next several days and write out what being who God has declared you to be should mean for the people around you. In the spaces below, reflect on your takeaways from each day of this devo. What has God taught you, and how will that change the way you live?

1. I am wonderfully knit together so that . . .

2. I am made in His image so that . . .

3. I am created with intention so that . . .

4. I am designed to be fruitful so that . . .

5. I am a tested teenager like Jesus so that . . .

6. I am His masterpiece so that . . .

7. I am where God lives so that . . .

8. I am reborn so that . . .

9. I am *actually* His child so that . . .

10. I am adopted by God so that . . .

11. I am filled with wonder so that . . .

12. I am not a slave to fear so that . . .

13. I am a child of a trustworthy Father so that . . .

14. I am a child of a Father I want to imitate so that . . .

15. I am "just-as-if-I never sinned" so that . . .

16. I am "just-as-if-I always obeyed" so that . . .

17. I am kept so that . . .

18. I am sealed so that . . .

19. I am victorious so that . . .

20. I am cleansed so that . . .

21. I am free so that . . .

22. I am His priest (part 1) so that . . .

23. I am His priest (part 2) so that . . .

24. I am in Christ so that . . .

25. I am His servant so that . . .

26. I am gifted so that . . .

27. I am a steward of His grace so that . . .

28. I am Christ's living letter so that . . .

29. I am a stranger so that . . .

30. I am not of the world so that . . .

31. I am a slave to righteousness so that . . .

32. I am a citizen of heaven so that . . .

33. I am transferred to the Kingdom of Light so that . . .

34. I am a new creation so that . . .

35. I am crucified to the world so that . . .

36. I am Christ's Ambassador so that . . .

37. I am His captive and fragrance so that . . .

38. I am His witness so that . . .

39. I am sent so that . . .

40. I am commissioned so that . . .

41. I am the salt of the earth so that . . .

42. I am the light of the world so that . . .

43. I am God's friend so that . . .

44. I am God's partner so that . . .

45. I am known by God so that . . .

46. I am deeply loved so that . . .

47. I am *with* Christ so that . . .

48. I am being conformed so that . . .

49. I am more than a conqueror so that . . .

Acknowledgments

Eric

I am very grateful for the team at Tyndale. Their commitment to Scripture, helping people encounter God's grace through books like this, and their excellence in their work is inspiring. Our editor, Danika Kelly, is amazing and made this devotional book better. I am also very grateful for our church, Mariners Church. Writing alongside Eden has been a deep joy, really a dream come true, and I know I am seeing the fruit of lots of people investing in her over her years in Mariners kids, junior high, and high school ministries. I feel the same about her teachers at Crockett, MCS, and Pacifica. Thank you!

Eden

It has been my greatest joy to be able to work with the Tyndale team. For my first experience going through the publishing process, I am so grateful for the way Tyndale has encouraged me and helped me bring my best to the book. Also, I am so grateful for my teachers (especially my high school teachers) who have prepared me so well and improved not only my ability to write, but my faith, my character, and my work ethic. It has been a privilege being able to write with my dad and spend even more quality time with him through this journey. I would like to thank Mariners Church, my second home, for caring so much for my family and rejoicing with us along the way as we wrote this book.

Notes

DAY 3

1. *Transgender Kids: Who Knows Best?*, produced by Sam Bagnall, directed by John Conroy (BBC, 2016), 39:29.

DAY 8

1. Warren Farrell and John Gray, *The Boy Crisis: Why Our Boys Are Struggling and What We Can Do About It* (BenBella Books, 2018), 105.

DAY 11

1. Jonathan Haidt, *The Anxious Generation: How the Great Rewiring of Childhood Is Causing an Epidemic of Mental Illness* (Penguin, 2024).

DAY 16

1. Nick Raguz, "When Stacey King Joked About His Contributions on Michael Jordan's Career-High Scoring Night," *Sports Illustrated*, November 11, 2023, https://www.si.com/nba/bulls/old-school/when-stacey-king-joked-about-his-contributions-on-michael-jordans-career-high-scoring-night.

DAY 34

1. C. S. Lewis, *Mere Christianity* (HarperOne, 2001), 216.

DAY 47

1. *Merriam-Webster Dictionary*, "hidden," accessed April 1, 2025, https://www.merriam-webster.com/dictionary/hidden.

About the Authors

Eric Geiger serves as the senior pastor of Mariners Church in Southern California, where he lives with his wife, Kaye, and their two daughters, Eden and Evie. Eric received his doctorate in leadership and church ministry from Southern Seminary. He loves investing in teenagers and young adults, recently serving as a high school guys group leader for four years and as the primary teacher of a young adult gathering.

Eden Geiger cowrote this devotional during her junior year after God's Word gripped her heart early in high school. Eden enjoys living in Southern California with her mom, dad, and sister, Evie. She loves the beach, hanging with friends, and serving kids with disabilities at church and through an organization she cofounded called Love Without Limits.

Your Feelings Aren't Weird

"Part workbook, part self-help guide, part Bible study, this handbook is geared toward those who experience big feelings and could use some support navigating the challenges that come with this territory. . . . Overwhelmed teens can find validation in this faith-based guide."
—*Kirkus Reviews*

CP1999

THE ORACLES OF FIRE SERIES

A faith-based fantasy
for YA readers set in the
Dragons in Our Midst story world

EYE OF THE ORACLE

ENOCH'S GHOST

LAST OF THE NEPHILIM

REFINING FIRES:
THE BONES OF MAKAIDOS, PART 1

FROM THE ASHES:
THE BONES OF MAKAIDOS, PART 2

CP2022